When the CHEERING Stops

Strategic Steps for Life After the Limelight

Kenny Randle

When The CHEERING Stops...

Copyright Page

Printed in

The United States of America

When the Cheering Stops

Written by Kenny Randle

ISBN: 978-0-578-37701-8

When The CHEERING Stops...

When The CHEERING Stops...

Dedication

I humbly and honorably dedicate this book to my wife Sonia.

"I will forever remember you planting the seed in my heart and in my thoughts to write this book, desiring me to tell the story of how I transitioned from a successful sports career, to my next field of play and competition in corporate America.

You dealt with all my starts and stops, ups and downs, and turnarounds and I could not have endured or done this without you"!

With enduring love and appreciation

Preface

Tbis book is about "transitioning," how to prepare for it, and how best to adapt. It deals with the diverse struggles of athletes, on and off the field. It speaks to the two deaths every athlete must die to and the pathway to choose after their sports career has ended.

The journey of a great athlete is quite unique. It almost always begins at a very young age, when they are influenced or impacted by sports figures they want to be like or admire.

It might stem from their parents, who were former athletes desiring to push their kids into their passion or gifting. It may also stem from coaches who recognize the talent they possess and desire to cultivate it and develop it to its maximum potential.

Unlike the casual weekend warrior or college intramural athlete, they have a relentless desire to be great. They go onto the court, field, and track to push themselves and pit themselves against the best. If they're good enough for the next level, they'll find that people will pay large sums of money to see them, touch them, and at times, live their fantasies or dreams through them.

When The CHEERING Stops...

Some even want to satisfy dreams of being around their "next level" athlete just to cheer their greatness!

You see, at one time, I was one of them. So I wrote this book to provide insight, consideration, advice or even direction to help prepare young athletes, especially *"When the Cheering Stops!"*

I felt moved to say what many athletes may feel uncomfortable saying or dealing with, particularly when they're in the prime of their athletic careers. There is a price for greatness, and every athlete that's ever accomplished anything noteworthy or legendary has always been willing to sacrifice and pay that price no matter the cost. They spill their blood, sweat, and tears on the courts and fields of play throughout their careers, but they don't want to arrive at the realization that their sports careers must one day come to an end.

Now, please understand, I wish that I could have played forever. If only these fragile bodies God gave us didn't have a "warranty/expiration date" on durability. But, as mentioned, the blood, sweat, and tears left on the field of play is, in the end, *"a simple single breath in time."*

Throughout this book, I periodically use biblical metaphors concerning sports. It's fantastic because the Apostle

Paul's biblical writings spoke a bit about his understanding and observation of athletes. ***"Running the race that is set before you" and the importance of athletes competing by the rules.*** **Hebrews 12:1; II Timothy 2:5**

I share them not only because I'm a Christian and a born-again believer but because I enjoy seeing people come from humble beginnings and circumstances rise to do great things through God's hands. So, I use them constantly in my small group meetings, sharing valuable insights toward our moving forward amidst great opposition and difficulty. An athlete's sports journey brings about many valuable life lessons.

My Pastor, Bishop T. D. Jakes, recently shared a message about people being able to "Mind Their Power" to move forward. His message prompted me to think about the athlete who must also learn to "mine their power." After it's over, the athlete has to be willing to dig down deep, as if mining for gold to find real wealth.

Allow me to share from experience that there is great value in developing a solid moral or God-directed spiritual compass for your life, laced with principles that stand the test of time. This will enable you to confront and withstand every challenge, circumstance, and situation you find yourself facing.

When The CHEERING Stops...

You might be at that stage in your athletic career where the "cheering has stopped," and need to parlay your skills into a productive enterprise. Know this: you are not meant to end up living life beneath your privilege and less than what God intended for you. *For He knows the plans He has for you, plans for your good, and not your detriment, to give you a future and a hope. Jer. 29:11*

Kenny Randle

Foreword By: Walter Bond

"When the Cheering Stops" is a must read for any athlete at any level or someone transiting out of the limelight. I know Kenny Randle the man, his spirit is genuine and his purpose on this earth is to be a living testimony of what can become of an athlete in their second act.

Kenny is honest and straightforward with what he shares in this book. He totally understands the assignment he has been divinely given. He is one of a few professionals that have the skill set and the heart to pull it off. Why? He did it himself, he left sports and has become a very successful executive after his cheering stopped.

A lot of authors will write about what they've heard, Kenny in this book is opening up the vessels of his own journey to empower athletes to make sure they pivot successfully as their cheering stops based on what he knows.

When The CHEERING Stops...

As a former professional athlete that has found success after my cheering stopped. I discovered other gifts on my own. If this book was in my hands from day one, I could have been spared the pain of my own transition out of sports and into my true purpose.

My sincere hope and expectation for the reader is to avoid incurring their own self-inflicted scars and make a smooth transition while using this brilliant book as their roadmap. Kenny Randle is a gem of a person and author, he absolutely nails it with this Masterpiece. The funny thing is, after this book is released we will never stop cheering on Kenny Randle and his efforts.

~ *Walter Bond*

Former NBA Player ~ Dallas Mavericks
Detroit Pistons-Utah Jazz
Collegiate player at Univ. of Minnesota
Certified Speaking Professional
Hall of Fame Speaker
Next Level Coach
www.BigSpeak.com

Acknowledgements

Most female athletes hit the peak of their careers at the collegiate level due to the lack of professional sports opportunities. Therefore, a book like this is of vital importance in preparing for that transition. In addition, I believe that tough and open conversations about this topic will help alleviate mental health issues that stem from not having the tools to cope with such a loss.

So thank you, Mr. Randle! Your book encouraged me to fulfill my purpose in reaching out to my female ***B-ball*** players to have these discussions.

When the Cheering Stops has a powerful message for athletes and their parents, I encourage you to read and share it with others!   *~Tulyah Gaines*

Former University of Notre Dame Women's Basketball Team Captain

Former Assistant coach San Bernardino Valley College Women's Basketball

Former director of Basketball operations The Penn State Lady Lions

When The CHEERING Stops...

"As a former collegiate and professional athlete, I found Kenny's book to be relatable, remarkable, and important in so many ways. Reading **"When the Cheering Stops!"** would have helped me immensely as I entered into the uncertain post-athletics world. Back then, like so many others both before and after me, I couldn't help but think, "What next?" Kenny's unique "YES model" provides a bridge for athletes to successfully transition to their future lives with confidence.

~ Charlie Ward

Former NBA Starter
Heisman Trophy and Davey O'Brien Award Winner
Won College Football National Championship

I am really grateful, honored and blessed to be able to give my acknowledgment to Kenny Randle on his new book entitled. *"When The Cheering Stops"* As my freshman college roommate at USC we all knew he was special not only on the field but his unique outlook on life and the Lord. His book *When the Cheering Stops* is a prime example of his caring nature and his commitment to serve and help others thank you Kenny Randle for such a wonderful book

~Danny Reece

USC Football Captain
Tampa Bay Buccaneers
NFL Record Holder: Led the National Football League in punt returns

When The CHEERING Stops...

Kenny's book **When the Cheering Stops** is a serious subject matter that must be addressed. I believe the world views athletes almost like gods, because of what they do on and off the field. When God gives someone a gift to excel at something, they ought to be able to be the best they can be at that thing.

What ends up happening is a fundamental disconnect between "when the cheering does stop" and the athlete's identity being linked to those cheers. It is almost like their whole personhood is derived from what they are saying in the media, the newspaper, or the magazines.

When the Cheering Stops can be an eye-opener for everyone. It's a book that will assist athletes in understanding what the accurate measure of applause means and where it needs to come from. More importantly it gives a realistic roadmap on where to go; **When the Cheering Stops**. (And believe me, it Will)

~ Vince Evans

Former NFL quarterback

Selected by the Chicago Bears in the 1977 NFL Draft.

Played at the University of Southern California

MVP of the 1977 Rose Bowl

When The CHEERING Stops...

I met Kenny Randle over 45 years ago as a rookie in Cleveland, as we both chased a dream of becoming a part of the fraternity of men in the National Football League. I was fortunate enough to have a 12-year career as a player becoming the 1st fulltime African American Punter so I have heard the cheers of fans and there is nothing like it.

The cheers of fans is like an Elixir that most players can't seem to get enough of. *"When the Cheering Stops"*, will take you on a journey that every player who has ever put on a NFL helmet, jersey or cleats has to face. Regardless if you only attend a training camp or if you had a 15 year Hall of Fame career, we all have to deal with the reality of what happens next in our lives.

I applaud Kenny for having the courage and ability to put into words this most difficult transition. One that every NFL player must face regardless of race, creed or color. One that begins *"When the Cheering Stops"*

~ Greg Coleman

12-year NFL Player ~ 1st African American NFL Punter

Black College Football Hall of Fame ~

Florida A & M University Football Hall of Fame

Sideline Analyst MN Vikings Radio Network

When The CHEERING Stops...

Kenny and I met early in our professional sports careers and were roommates for a short time. This was in the late 1970's; our team was riding the wave of two Super Bowl appearances and it was a heady time for two young men.

The Future looked bright and exciting and while we talked about life after football, we had no concrete game-plan. Kenny has touched upon an important concept with this missive. His unique tale of his life path could be the inspiration for a new generation of athletes.

This book **When The Cheering Stops** is an excellent playbook for that college or pro athlete that is ready to transition out of sports and enter their next position in life.

~ *Tony Hill*

Former NFL wide receiver

Played ten seasons for the Dallas Cowboys.

Played college football at Stanford University.

When The CHEERING Stops...

"Every great leader must understand that success is not about shinning in the spotlight, it's about preparing for the next phase of life.

Kenny Randle lays out in powerful detail the mindset and game plan that we all need to embrace when we transition from one phase to another.

This book is a blueprint to prepare us all with the insights and tools we need to overcome any challenge and succeed, no matter what the competition may bring. I'm honored to call him friend.

~ *Anton J. Gunn* MSW, CSP

Former SEC Offensive Lineman
Former senior advisor to Barack Obama
Healthcare Leadership Consultant

"Kenny has hit the nail on the head with, "When The Cheering Stops" ! He's individually experienced what it's like to be a big time athlete, and compete at the highest levels, then having to shift when it all stops and then use his skills and talents to carve a pathway for success into another realm of competition.

Charles W. Lee

(Central high School football/track coach,

Running back coach University of TX-1977-1981,

Director of Relations Denver Broncos -1981-1998

Part 1: Mentoring for the Transition

The Fatherless Child

E veryone gathered around the gravesite to say their final goodbyes, everyone, except me. It was a beautiful October day, but a sorrowful time indeed. My father died of brain cancer just a few days before I was born. As my daddy was lowered into the cold ground, my mother, a very young and grieving wife, went into labor with me. She was rushed across town from the cemetery to a country hospital and gave birth to me.

I never viewed my father's death as losing him because I never had any recollection of him. As a child, all I wished for was to have known my father to play catch with him, go fishing or hunting or just be by his side. Fatherlessness leaves you vulnerable as a young boy. It can allow you to go places and do things that can get you in a lot of trouble. I was fortunate to have a strong God- fearing mother and extended male family network to bridge some of that gap.

I guess the pain of not knowing my father was better than knowing him and then having to say goodbye as a little boy. It made me realize how much sons truly need their fathers.

Ask any man that has ventured through the maze of his life without a father figure and he'll tell you that one of the greatest deficits he had along his journey was the lack of a mentor and someone to model manhood for him.

Kenny Randle

Dr. Ed Cole, the forerunner of the Christian Men's Ministry movement back in the '80s, said, "In life, we are either entering or leaving." My father left this life, and I entered. I didn't tell you this story to gain sympathy. Although I grew up without a father, my family constantly told me stories about him, including his love, character, and personality. Fortunately, I heard about the good things, for they never spoke of his bad qualities, challenges, or shortcomings.

As a little boy, my Aunt and Uncle would always introduce me to other people by saying "this is Kenneth's son" because my father was well known to many in the small country town of

Richmond, Missouri. Everyone I met in that little town would say, "Your father was very a good man—an honest man!"

Those statements always made me proud because I think I was looking for some connection with my father, in a picture, in a story, anything. It made me -deep down inside, want to be a good and honest man, too.

I never got to know his touch, feel his strength, or hear his words, but I never counted it as misfortune or lack because the love I was given always helped fill the gap.

I didn't realize until the last few years that I probably dealt with some level of abandonment issues and didn't know it. Even though it wasn't my father's fault, I still felt it. I had tremendous love and support around me, yet I realized that not having him but wanting that father figure caused me to become an overachiever wishing to become or be somebody special one day.

I tried hard to make up for his absence through other role models I respected, wanting them to see my accomplishments and hoping they were proud of me. I was always looking for some connection.

When The CHEERING Stops...

Developing My Passion

I often recall those hot, sweltering summer days when heat waves bounced off the asphalt pavement as all the neighborhood kids gathered around our local spot to play pick-up baseball in the church parking lot. We were hidden by chest-high green hedges elevated above the traffic of the city streets below.

We were never without a plan, whether we played a single game, double or triple header that took us into nightfall. Like the time we played two hard-fought baseball games and ended up in a one-to-one tie. Afterward, we took a short break, ran home, scarfed down our dinner, and went back outside for one more game to determine the winner before nightfall.

Of course, when it was summer, we got to stay out past sundown, which was about 8:30 at night. Now I know how ridiculous that might sound if you're a kid growing up today. Still, we had to be plenty creative in our neighborhood when games went past sundown. To finish our doubleheaders, we would bust the lock (*oops, I meant*, open up the light switch box) in the church lot (*yes, I said church parking lot)*, turned on the lights, and continue playing until we finished.

When The CHEERING Stops...

It was a real big deal for us. We really thought we were doing something big time. At least until one of the church deacons came into the lot yelling and shouting how bad we were and chased us off the lot.

I have to admit that breaking off the padlock to the light switch box in the church parking lot was pretty rogue of us at the time. I guess we figured it kept us off the streets, and surely something so small wouldn't get us in trouble with God. We believed He wouldn't be mad at a bunch of neighborhood kids who were just having a little summertime fun,

These times were some of the most memorable moments of my life. Little did I realize that these fun-filled childhood escapades would serve as the launching pad of my love affair with sports.

There was nothing like playing, competing and trying to outdo each other, whether baseball, football, or racing through the neighborhood streets. It didn't matter where we played on a sandlot or public street. There was always something hypnotic about competing in sports.

Many years have gone by, the lot looks a lot smaller, the bushes have withered away, and the homes have fallen apart. Yet, the images, sounds, and memories of those days in the parking lot will always be indelibly etched in my mind and heart, never withering away. This was the beginning of my life in sports.

Whether it was in the heat of the day or the cool of a late fall with yellowish-brown and tan leaves covering every blade of grass in the area, we made our way to that asphalt parking lot. It had no name. We just called it "the parking lot."

It was surrounded by three one-foot, perfectly manicured shrubs, aligned with neighborhood houses that, with just a little imagination, would cause us to envision standing in Wrigley Field or Red Sox Stadium in Boston. But we weren't.

Instead, we were smack dab in the middle of the hood, dreaming and pretending that thousands of fans were watching us hit a fastball out of the park or catch the winning touchdown with screaming fans cheering us.

There were no organized sports teams in my area when I was young. Instead, those were reserved for the older high school boys that played on teams sponsored by local Boys Clubs, mortuaries, or hardware stores, with the team pictures found on the back of paper fans with wooden handles used during church service at every black church in town.

We were never without our idols. We kept them close, stored in our back jean pockets in the form of trading cards. There

24

were no iPhones or smartphones to recall their latest stats. Yet, we talked about them as if we knew them personally and acted as if they were part of us. You see, they were our heroes, and in some cases, our uncles, brothers, or even fathers who pioneered the road before us!

We would talk about our dreams of one day striking it rich and getting paid while trading baseball cards and reviewing the stats of our heroes.

During the summers, you could always find us on the weekends with baseball bats and gloves, at least those who could afford them. We were imitating our heroes, players that, for most of us, only existed on baseball cards, radio, or NBC once a week.

The parking lot was our neighborhood sports complex because it doubled as our football-baseball stadium, depending on the season. It was our get-a-way from the streets, crime, and foolishness and allowed us to dream *"One day I could be like...."*

It was here that we imagined the crowds roaring, screaming, and cheering, long before we ever experienced it in our own lives. You know what? It didn't matter. We were kids, and all we thought about was the love of the game. .

When The CHEERING Stops...

Not a Game for the Faint-hearted

"I'm not playing with you, sucker. Now throw the damn ball right, or I'm going to throw this bat upside your head," Alvin demanded, as he waited over and over again for what he believed to be the "perfect pitch" from Robert Earl, our neighborhood pitcher, and block comedian.

Alvin stood there with his burly body, raising and swinging his bat high in the air, talking smack, swearing at us, as he crowded home plate. You see, Alvin was our neighborhood bully. He had to have everything go his way, or else you felt the wrath of his anger, verbally and sometimes physically, depending on if he half liked you. Not a comforting thought for someone trying to make it through an already rough neighborhood.

On the other hand, Robert was a tall, lanky, perfectionist when it came to the art of throwing. He threw everything straight—rocks, baseballs, even snowballs in the winter. He was the master at it, and everyone playing that day knew he would never give Alvin the satisfaction of hitting one of his pitches out of the parking lot!

Then, all of a sudden, without warning. ***WOOOOSH!***

When The CHEERING Stops...

You could hear the wind whisking from that Louisville slugger baseball bat as it left Alvin's grip. It spun end over end, heading straight towards Robert Earl's head, but at the very last second, Robert Earl ducked, extending his arm high in the air as a shield. Then CRACK! The bat connected with his wrist, and fear surrounded us, knowing he was hurt real bad, but selfishly thinking it was the beginning of the end for our best pitcher in the neighborhood.

Well, the best part of this story was that Robert's wrist was not broken but badly bruised and swollen. But the worst part was that we had to keep playing because any athletic contest the older boys played in, any water breaks or injury timeouts, was decided by them, and not the young pups that were coming up behind them.

The older guys felt that it was *"their job to grow us up"* and ensure that we didn't turn out to be mama's boys. So, if there were guys in the neighborhood who were soft, and I'm sure that there were some, it was taboo to show it, or you were teased unmercifully, or better yet, faced a beat down!

Needless to say, after that day, nobody volunteered for the pitcher's job at The Parking Lot when Alvin came around! Butwe loved every minute of growing up in the hood and wouldn't have traded it for anything in the world.

Shaping Me

It was probably right before my first year in Junior High School (also known as Middle School) when I began to realize that I might have a thumbnail of unproven and underdeveloped athletic talent. I felt like I had arrived because it was a long way from the black and grey asphalt "parking lot" to playing on the grass at the Kansas City Parks and Recreation Summer League.

There was a renowned park in the neighborhood called Central Park, where all the up-and-coming neighborhood athletes played. There were no organized or sponsored teams, so we just showed up and played. Of course, there would be the mixed group of local and well-known teenage thugs and hoodlums that held court there, and they decided who played and who didn't play!

The plain truth is these guys I hung out with my last summer before entering Junior High School were decent athletes. They were fun to be around when we were shooting pool, hitting a softball, or swimming at the local YMCA. However, anything other than that meant hanging out with them at your own risk!

They lacked the very essence of what it took to be involved in a team environment, discipline!

There were only two choices to enjoy playing summer sports at this level in my area. Either you joined their hand-selected teams and played well (shades of Robert "the pitcher" Earl), or you didn't go to Central Park.

Gang rules were, if you didn't play with the gang, you didn't play. They were the represented team for Park and Recreation. If you didn't play, you got ostracized and would eventually have to fight someone to justify your reason for hanging around. These gang leaders were bullies and came from chaotic homes. Yet my desire to play sports and test my skills was so strong it overruled the probable consequences. When school resumed in the fall, I left that group far behind because many were dropouts, and I had new territory to explore.

We were in an era where there were few, if any, little league-sponsored teams or anything organized for us to participate...

It's funny, today as an adult, I find myself going into these same neighborhoods ministering, encouraging, and evangelizing to lost and hurting kids needing a connection just like myself. Many of these young people are hurting, disenfranchised, and disenchanted with life. They represent many of the young black urban youth in the inner city that I've had the opportunity to reach out to, who often see their world in only a five-block radius because they feel it's the one area they can manage and control. Most live in a haunted house and want out but don't know exactly how to break away.

My first exposure to organized sports came on the first week of Junior High School during swim period. It wasn't just any swim period. It was the most whispered and intimidating event to come in a young boy's life. The entire 7th-grade class was required to swim without our clothes. It seems weird in retrospect because it caused huge self-consciousness issues and peer pressure for 12-13-year-old boys.

When the day came, we found out that it wasn't a rumor, but like an initiation or some sort of embarrassing and intimidating rite of passage. I'm sure that today all the coaching staff in the school would be fired.

Incidents like this blur the line between acceptable and out of bounds. Growing up can be tough, and it gets even tougher as an athlete. This event and others introduced kids to the spectrum of interscholastic chaos in the hood. It was somehow a protected environment in that it was all males. Nonetheless, being exposed like that was more than a bit intimidating.

Growing Up

As I look back into the events and stages of my boyhood, and teen years, I recognize that I was truly blessed. We didn't have all that we wanted, and I know for a fact my mother constantly overextended herself financially, attempting to provide for us. But I was surrounded by a family that genuinely supported and loved one another, something very unique compared to what we experience in today's society. It wasn't always pretty growing up, and at times life was a lonely and insecure place that could get ugly and even perverted at times. Growing up with no fatherly direction or counsel is the very reason many youth and young adults get lost in the shuffle today, with over 50% of homes without fathers in the household.

Thank God for a strong mother who loved her children. Although two of the four kids each had different fathers (because of my mother remarrying twice) we knew no difference between half brother or sister. We were all family who loved and cared for one another greatly. My mother didn't hesitate to bring swift and hard correction to straighten us up, when we got out of line which was often, except my older sister Bonnie.

When The CHEERING Stops...

For me, it was all a part of growing up in the hood wasn't always pretty. In fact, at times, it got "downright ugly" growing up, without a father and having a single mother. Especially in an environment that didn't care whether you succeeded, failed, or became a statistic.

It may have deepened when I began spending my summers in the country with my Aunt Fannie and Uncle Percy. He and I worked on Calvert's Farm in Richmond, MO. After he would come home from working 8-10 hour days as a maintenance man at the local high school, we would go to work on the farm. He would pay me part of the small wages he earned as a farmhand, to teach me the value of work and reward.

My Uncle Percy was a rugged, strong, and soft-spoken man. He was also the last person in the world you wanted to cross or to get mad because he was strong as an ox.

As hard as he worked and as tired as he got, I never heard him complain about work. So guess what? He indirectly taught me that you don't complain about work. You just put your hand to the plow and do it! This was the foundation developed within me on "purpose" and accounts for the strong work ethic that I possess today.

What does that have to do with sports? Well, I'm glad you asked. Most think that superstar athletes are naturally talented and gifted, and that's correct. Still, the ones in the upper echelon that stay there year after year have a great work ethic (i.e. Tiger Woods, which I'll discuss in another chapter).

I will never forget Hall of Famer Wide Receiver Jerry Rice's story about being a bricklayer with his father in the summer. He spoke of how tedious, laborious, and specific the work he did with his father was each day. Not only did that work build physical strength, but it was also creating a level of precision in his life. Jerry was a renowned perfectionist by all those around him on the field of play. He understood that you couldn't take shortcuts or cut corners. He attributed his greatness to getting the bricks perfectly aligned. It crafted a mental mindset shift that caused him to see those patterns as a degree of perfectionism.

Full of Dreams and Ambition

While growing up, I arose each day full of dreams, imagination, and desire to be something more. Like most young boys in my day, I grew up wanting to be an astronaut, a doctor, an attorney. Yes, an attorney. It was viewed with much less contempt because of the level of oppression going on in this country that black people faced. Anyone who represented someone to level the playing field or bring about fairness was revered. And like most kids, I always dreamed of being or doing something great one day. But I knew there was more for me than what I was experiencing in my neighborhood.

OVERCOMING is the only word to describe my many childhood situations and outcomes. It has always been my M.O. (*modus operandi*). I always tried to move on and not dwell upon my lacks: lack of money, lack of resources, lack of mentors, or lack of experience. Instead, I made up for it with DESIRE!

Most families in my neighborhood didn't sit around at the dinner table discussing economics, community improvement or our highs in the stock market... We discussed surviving and tightening the belt, hoping that my mom would keep her job working for the wealthy family whose house she cleaned and cooked for every other day.

You see, I was the diamond in the rough, the good kid in an uncertain place, surrounded by negative influences and temptations. I was like some kids today but with fewer choices, fewer creature comforts, and no Google, Instagram, Facebook or Tik Tok.

When The CHEERING Stops...

In the Bible, there is a story of twelve spies sent into enemy territory to spy out the land and size up the people. Ten spies came back with a negative report and stated that the inhabitants of the land were so daunting that the spies looked like grasshoppers in their sight! Although we didn't have all we wanted growing up, we never viewed ourselves as "grasshoppers!"

Living with Less

We may not have had a lot growing up, but we didn't view it as lack, and we were content. We knew our Mothers would do what they could to provide. The same held true with our schools. So whether it was hand-me-down football jerseys we wore, given to us by a nearby military academy, or having a weight room with only a few weights that we kept under lock and key, we were content. Nevertheless, we thought we had won the lottery just by having any sports equipment or uniforms at all. To us, we looked like the hero's we saw on TV, and it didn't matter that it was used. They were NEW to us, and we acted like they were brand new. That's the epitome of contentment.

We understood who we were and the nature of our environment. We accepted that we lacked the financial resources or conveniences our counterpart suburban schools took for granted. As little kids playing the game of counting how many

35

Whites drove their cars through our communities, we never saw them living in our areas. Truthfully, this was a time of segregated life, based primarily on socio-economic conditions rather than racial biases.

I suppose we didn't give much thought to our situation because as Black families, we were survivors. In those days, our parents were hard-working people, blue-collar workers for the most part, with a desire to see their children have better. But not so far removed as our young people are today in not recognizing the value of having a work ethic.

Our families found a way to make it, even if it meant borrowing money from Aunties or Grandmas. Often there wasn't something special on the table we wanted to eat but we ate what was served, or we didn't eat! This fostered and shaped a profound sense of appreciation and an attitude of gratitude in many former successful athletes. It was a different mindset.

Test of Manhood

Growing up in the streets on the east side of Kansas City was no joke. It was difficult at times, but it let you see that most people can adapt to the environments and situations thrown their way, even when they didn't choose to be a part of it. I didn't decide to grow up without a father in the house. My father didn't choose to die of a brain tumor. It wasn't by choice that my mom went into labor at the gravesite. She was rushed to a hospital across the Missouri River several miles across town because we had no hospital in our community that serviced African Americans.

I was born into an era vastly different than today. Even the bad kids had been given more foundation and God-centered principles in my childhood than we find today. I wouldn't classify myself as a hard individual or "bad boy," but I grew up around hard people in a challenging area. We call it the inner city today, but it was called the ghetto when I grew up. The ghetto made way a lot of time for testing and preparing you for the realities of life.

For example, kids trying to fill the void from divorce, separation, emotional trauma, drugs, alcohol, crime, abuse, and dysfunctional families were constantly hanging out together playing sports. Sports allowed us to have a level of escapism from the daily pressures. These same circumstances exist today, except it now encompasses families of all cultures. Consequently, kids in these circumstances can't seem to find a way to channel their aggression and pain that gets bottled up inside. So they usually find one of two outlets, sports or crime. Right about now, you're telling me, "Kenny, that's stereotyping." You're right. That's the pressure I spoke of earlier.

When The CHEERING Stops...

That's what I spent a large part of my athletic career working to change. I try to make a difference every time I have a chance. At the beginning of my sales career, I recall never sharing with a prospective client that I was a former pro athlete. I wanted to dispel the negative stereotypes and perceptions often ascribed to African American athletes. I wanted them to accept me on my abilities as a business equivalent, not as a former jock. In the same breath, I can tell you that many successful athletes come out of well-disciplined, God-fearing families with traditional values.

As a mentor and life coach myself, it's evident that many of our young men today have a warped concept of being a man. Why? Because they are being talked about yet not taught.

As I write this book, my intention is not to exclude the many women or young female athletes reading this book. Female athletes have similar pressures, issues, and adjustments to make when the cheering stops in their lives too, yet I have found that women are better at expressing their emotions than most men. And what usually transpires is that women explode by letting it all out, and men implode by keeping it all inside.

For many young people in this country, sports is not only a way of life; it IS their life! It's a way out of a dingy, cramped roach-infested apartment. It's an escape from a drug-infested neighborhood where they are propositioned every day to sample their wares.

For many, it is a vehicle to get mama out of that hard life she's had and repay her for the sacrifices she's made. But for most, it's the love of the game, competing, growing, accomplishing, and becoming something or someone, and a great way of developing greatness and accomplishment in their life. It's a way to become somebody respected and create a pathway out of their existing circumstances and issues for something better.

Sports becomes the vehicle, the catalyst, the conduit that our young athletes use to live their dreams, attain their hopes, and fuel their aspirations. You might be saying at this point many families are not like the ones I have been describing. Well, you're right, but I know many families that have these challenges, and I must write about it. I must expose the deficiencies so others appreciate how they overcame great obstacles to obtain unprecedented dreams and success in sports and in life.

These behaviors have a lot to do with the attitudes and mindsets that have been cultivated and developed in our children Movies, magazines, sports, and media hype can paint an unrealistic picture. Young athletes face many external forces out of their control. They're pulled at, tugged at, and daily reminded that fantasy is much better than reality!

Mentoring - The Missing Link

Athletes are an interesting bloodline. First, there are so many successful and accomplished athletes in this world, many who have reached great heights and who have had to overcome tremendous challenges in their lives by just sheer dogged determination.

These athletes pushed or willed themselves to heights of success in their field and came out on top. If they were fortunate, they were mentored by a coach, a parent, or maybe even another athlete, who became their connection or example and a guidepost to success.

Unfortunately, a number of athletes today have gotten A+ on the field of play but may have flunked miserably in the classroom of life. So the result has caused many "athletic casualties of war" living in ignorance and defiance.

In today's ***what-have-you-done-for-me-lately*** world of athletics, it seems that once you're done performing and giving you're all making the university or pro team rich, they begin looking for "who's next?" That's why it is important that today's generation of athletes have a strategy and not rest on their laurels.

When The CHEERING Stops...

In other words, have a plan to implement your plan. It's not enough to have thoughts and dreams of success. You must craft a plausible plan to be able to execute your dreams. Just being strong or fast is not nearly good enough. There will always be bigger, stronger, faster competitors than yourself out. Today's top athletes work relentlessly to train, prepare and condition themselves to compete and be the best possible. They must also train their mindset on being the absolute best, which is the ticket to get you in the door. So your Plan "B" must be that your Plan "A" has to work.

Part 2: Confronting Our Mortality

Dying Two Deaths

As athletes living in a Western sports culture, the very last chapter we want to read is our athletic timeline—our sports epitaph—which requires us to one day hang up the cleats, shoes, sticks, or rackets.

An athlete lives and breathes his sport for the love of the game, the roar of the crowd, and all the enticing? Fringe benefits. If they are fortunate enough to reach pro status, they will do anything legal and sometimes illegal to preserve, extend or enhance that athletic life.

This creates blind spots for the 21st-century athlete who is faster, stronger, and bigger than previous generations. We are a part of a culture that believes in being seen, heard, and felt. When performance is weakened, we believe there must be a potion, pill, surgery, or shot that can fix it.

Staying Relevant!

Everyone wants to be relevant today. Some athletes will slowly die for the love of the sport and the roar of the crowd. The prevalent use of steroids today is a great example. Unfortunately, people unknowingly, or knowingly sometimes, risk their lives with the long-term effects of performance-enhancing drug usage. Take Marion Jones, one incredibly gifted athlete. At the 2000 Olympic Games she became the first woman to win five track and field medals at a single Olympics. In an effort to stay on top, she used banned substances and had to return the medals. She was willing to risk it all and did so, colliding with failure.

They are warriors obsessed with the love of the game and the battle of competition. They don't want to see tomorrow or be reminded that the end will come soon.

Athletes spend their lives competing and performing all while enveloping and insulating the cheers of adoring fans and loving family.

I remember it as though yesterday, on the sidelines on injured reserve with the Cowboys. We were in Miami to play Super Bowl XIII. This game was a rematch against the Pittsburgh Steelers, winners of two previous Super Bowls against the Cowboys.

Terry Bradshaw, star quarterback for the Steelers, had one of his most prolific games, throwing for over 356 yards.

When The CHEERING Stops...

Unfortunately, we lost the game 35 to 31. The winners got the lion's share of the money, and the losers got the loser's pay.

There was one scene I will never forget in my short stint with pro-football. The official's gun signaled the end of battle for the NFL's best, and as I stood next to the bench, I remember the sight of two perennial All-Pro players, sitting on the bench among half-empty buckets of Gatorade, arm pads, and blood-stained tape. They were blankly staring at the field with tears starting to roll down their cheeks.

You see, the end of the game wasn't only about the money (although $20,000 was a lot of money in that day), but it was about their love for the game and the desire to go out as a winner! They knew they were saying goodbye to the sport they had given so much to and that had given so much to them.

You might say, isn't that a bit extreme? After all, it's only a game. Well, imagine spending your life since childhood in a highly competitive sport, and there were no options to inherit the family business or go to a college unless you had an athletic scholarship?

Your *only* way out of the struggle of your parent's ghetto was with a scholarship, and that meant countless hours learning, practicing, sacrificing, and often pushing yourself to the breaking point of mental and physical exhaustion.

Then, upon finally reaching a pinnacle of success in the sport, having then to be forced through physical injury and limitations to *die to the thing that gave so much life, stature, confidence, and identity.*

The athlete must slowly die. Passion, pride, and satisfaction must shift to the stands, coaching, or even the cable TV channels.

The athlete is the only person who dies two deaths, once to their sport and the second to himself.

The athlete's death is a slow process because they must die to that which bought them a life of self-worth, identification, and exposure.

The successful and visionary athlete must have in their side-view mirror other areas that can be explored that create passion, accomplishment, and success. Whether it's staying connected to their sport through coaching, counseling or if very fortunate, the rare sports commentating.

The First Death

At some point, the athlete's career must live through *the death of his sport.*

When The CHEERING Stops...

Memories linger on in an athlete. He never forgets the images, sounds, euphoria and disappointments, sometimes painful and pleasurable.

Being in organized sports most of my life, I had the pleasure of playing with and competing against some of the most gifted and brilliant athletes in the world. We spent our lives competing and performing in stadiums, basketball courts, and fields, testing our skills against one another, and enveloping ourselves in the cheers of adoring fans.

We started as youngsters trying to impress our parents, teachers, and those around us by performing or trying to impress those who showed the slightest amount of interest or approval in our ability to amuse and excite a crowd. But, hey, that's what kids do. They perform!

Consequently, athletes live for the *"roar of the crowd"* and the joy of competition. Still, unfortunately, when cheers come to an end, it can become difficult for athletes to admit that their lives in sports are over, particularly if they were fortunate to achieve a level of greatness or even stardom.

Many are left standing still, pondering their future, and asking themselves, "What do I do now?" "Where do I go from here?" These were the questions I asked myself on many occasions when I wasn't sure what was to become of my life after sports.

Yes, when athletes and performers die to their sport or craft, they tend to hold on to what was, which can be emotional and traumatic. **"*In The Bible, King Solomon wrote "to every time there is a season, a time to live, and time to die..."*** He wrote only God knows the appointed time. The football jock doesn't know. The basketball, soccer, and track athlete doesn't know. All athletes live their sports day in and day out unconcerned about the expiration of it. I can tell you firsthand that athletic success and accomplishment are an addiction like no other. The focus is on just one more season, one more quarter or one more play, one more opportunity to be in the atmosphere of competition and camaraderie!

Unfortunately, the day comes when they must die to the passion they pursued and cultivated over a lifetime. It's usually a lifelong dream that has driven them daily since childhood. They ate it, drank it, dreamed about it, and thought about it each waking moment. Many loved the competitiveness, teamwork, and life lessons they learned as a result of having an athletic career.

When The CHEERING Stops...

Ultimately, athletes must ask the question, "Will I be prepared to die to it so I can ultimately live successfully and move forward?"

"Unless a grain of wheat falls to the ground and dies, it stands alone, but if it dies, it brings forth much fruit."-

The Apostle John

In my experience of working with athletes, if you don't surrender or die to self, you may find yourself in a constant flux of uncertainty, thinking about what was, or what could have been your future.

In my experience, those who aren't willing to surrender or die to their sports find themselves in a constant flux of uncertainty, pondering about what could have or should have been their future.

They are like a driver who continues to check their rearview mirror. That slowly hinders momentum towards what's ahead.

When The CHEERING Stops...

You might say, "But it's only a game?" To an athlete it is more than a game. They hang on to a thread of hope that they still have one more chance to advance,

"There's MORE on the Menu"

When my wife and I were newly married, we always had a truckload of passion and love but a thimble full of money. This would often cause us to eat out at places with caution, always reading the menu from right to left, constantly concerned about the cost!

I recall her brother Fred being with us on those occasions, and within a millisecond of scanning the menu, he would say, "Cheeseburger and French fries please!"

I asked him one night why he ordered the same thing over and over again, and he said, "Well, nobody can mess up a cheeseburger, so it's a safe bet!" But one night after witnessing his ceremony of ordering food, I blurted out from the table, "Fred, you do know there's more on the menu!" Hey there athlete, "There is more on the menu, more dragons to slay, more challenges to take on, and accomplishments to fulfill beyond the sport." We become so ingrained and permanently weaved in our sports psyche and lives that we never want to come to grips with an ending.

If that rings true with you, start reading the menu from "left to right" and stop worrying about <u>the cost of the unknown</u>. You didn't operate that way when developing yourself for your sport. There is more to accomplish. The practice of being open to more will allow you to enjoy each moment and teach you to look forward to the NEXT!

It was the summer of my junior year at USC, and I had just posted the fastest time in the world for the 400 meters that year. I was anxious to go to Europe that summer and challenge myself by competing internationally against some of the world's best runners.

Europe was the ultimate opportunity for a U.S. track & field athlete at that time. It was a known fact that European fans greatly revered and appreciated U.S. sprinters, partly due to the scarcity of European talent in the sprint events.

That experience was an athlete's dream, competing, traveling, and exploring new worlds as a "wet around the ears" college athlete that had never traveled abroad.

I competed in London, Paris, Italy, and Sweden for four weeks, experiencing wonderful people and beautiful countries. I attribute this to shaping my ability to embrace diverse races, cultures, and languages.

My journey was somewhat gypsy-like, traveling within Europe from city to city, leaving athletic bags I had been given in hotel rooms because they were too small to carry all the gear shoe companies wanted me to wear. I had to arrange my travel with event track meet promoters from one competition to another.

The terms for competing were that my flight back to the States would be paid for if I won, and if I didn't, well, that was an option I could not afford to entertain. To get to my first stop in Europe to compete, I had to negotiate thru an Olympian friend for a one-way ticket to run the 400 meters in Milan, Italy's great sports coliseum. But, as you might guess, it was the greatest level of motivation for winning you could ever imagine!

Being in sales for many years now, I often look back on my time running in Europe. My experience negotiating my travel was exciting, particularly as a carefree college athlete, because it taught me how to *always sell myself first before selling my product!*

I knew that my family would be very proud of me when returning home. Only my family members in the military had ever traveled outside the country. I was on top of the world. So just like an excited kid, the first move I made when I arrived back in my hometown of Kansas City was to grab my mother's white Honda sedan and get back to my old neighborhood. I wanted to connect with Daniel Stanley, my absolute best friend in the world!

Dan was one of those friends every dude wished that he had in his life. He was loyal, trustworthy, a secret keeper, and cool as the day is long! We were typical best buds, which meant we kept all our secrets and shenanigans to ourselves. Swearing as brothers to "tell no one, under any circumstances" what we contrived, cooked up, and snuck past our mothers.

Outside of being best friends, there was one thing that genuinely cemented our friendship, and that was sports. We loved playing and talking sports, sometimes even more than being with the ladies. Now don't get me wrong, the girls in school always got our attention, but sports was our first love!

The way I saw it, getting an athletic college scholarship was my total everything. It was my ticket and rite of passage out of the hood.

Dan never was offered the opportunity to go to college on a sports scholarship, yet he was a hardworking dude, and a crazy competitor. Other kids told me that his basketball skills helped him have hands ideal for catching footballs, but I had the advantage of being blessed with speed.

He would say things like, "Man, if I had your speed Bub, I would have been the Second Coming Hall of Fame All-time great, KC Chief's Otis Taylor."

You see, we didn't grow up in the cable TV era where you could access pro-sports 24/7 and see your coveted heroes. Instead we had to dream and emulate them in neighborhood parking lots, playgrounds, or unlevel break-your-neck concrete basketball courts.

Fortunately, my successes in sports never got in the way of our friendship. We came from similar places, raised in single-parent homes with little extra money. We had mothers that were hard workers that scuffed and scraped to provide and guide us as best they could in our wild, crazy, crime-filled neighborhoods.

Although we had our own unique set of struggles, we would never change or exchange those moments to this day. Because they were the fuel needed for the dreams and determination forged in our hearts to become and do more with our lives.

We were always dreamers. We believed and held on to the vision of doing well enough in sports to springboard out of our neighborhood into another realm of success. We planned to show everyone that you can make it and become something greater.

It was during those dream-building moments that I would tell myself, "if I ever made it big, whether in the Olympics or Pro Football, my family and close friends would share all the swag that sports success could offer an athlete from the tough neighborhoods of Kansas City."

Dan and I took great pride in the loyalty we shared for one another. We would protect and encourage each other through the difficult experiences we faced. We were friends and brothers who were definitely "dream chasers."

Although the cheering stopped in Dan's sports life after high school, he didn't walk away upset, bitter, or worried about the future. He knew that colleges were not coming to knock at his door, but he always enjoyed, respected, and honored the game for what it gave him, "an opportunity to compete" and be a part of a tremendous high school legacy. He accepted that and proudly went forward. I respected the hell out of him for his determination and attitude.

The summers were full of close families and childhood friends hangin' out in my neighborhood, and countless memories that we would carry with us always.

When The CHEERING Stops...

Sometimes it read like daily crime reports, *"Man three doors down, shot dead,"* or *"former athlete's body found, expected foul play"* or *"city corruption at an all-time high, no sign of immediate change."*

So living on our playground was about self-preservation and survival. It wasn't sitting at the dinner table discussing investment strategies or summer vacation spots. Instead, my mother would encourage us with words of how God would keep us and "make a way" for us if we placed our trust in Him and not man.

My Biblical references were birthed from our God-fearing families who wanted more for their children. I understood the sacrifices being made for me so I could make something of myself.

Regardless of the city's social temperature, I always enjoyed my visits home because it made me feel connected to my roots. It also let others know that I didn't get lost in the shuffle as some coaches and haters predicted during my ascension into bigtime college sports! I wanted to appreciate and visibly be a positive representation to those who had trained me, raised me, and built a bridge for me to walk across.

When The CHEERING Stops...

Legends in Their Own Mind

Many great athletes came out of my hometown of Kansas City. But just like most cities at that point in time, we came from good, hardworking families with strong values, instilled with hope from our parents to go higher and further than themselves.

Yet still, there were life circumstances and situations that were ever-present in our neighborhoods, such as poverty, societal problems, dysfunctional family issues, ongoing incarceration, and a lack of opportunities for young black males like myself.

Many of us got our athletic start growing up and hanging out at the neighborhood Boys Club or YMCA. But as valuable as they were for shaping and molding marginalized kids, they are rapidly becoming a thing of the past.

You see, growing up in neighborhoods like mine, you were usually identified by the block you lived on and the kids that occupied that block. Whether it was 39th street, 32nd street, 12th street projects, or 42nd street, each had its characteristics and flavor. On my block, we were identified by sports. It was the air we breathed, the dreams we envisioned, and the competitive spirit we fostered for future greatness.

When The CHEERING Stops...

Returning home was always a great feeling. My neighborhood roots reminded me of the many obstacles I had to overcome to make it out. I could have easily been swallowed up as a statistic. But, having little resources and big dreams made me hungry to be something, do something and have something more. So much so that I was willing to pay a premium price to obtain it.

It began when I earned a football/track scholarship to the University of Southern California (USC). Of course, it felt good to receive accolades and acknowledgment from the newspapers, coaches, and well-wishers. Even the haters took pride in my accomplishments. That's just one of the funny things about human nature. If you make it, they can brag about knowing you in some form or fashion. In a sense, witnessing success in another athlete's life, career, or succeeding at another level can remind you of what you once hoped to achieve.

At the end of my freshman year of college, I made my trek back home to Kansas City. I was ready to see old friends, share good times with the family, and just work out.

My second day home, I could hardly wait to drive down 35th and Indiana and breathe in the sights and sounds of the old neighborhood.

When The CHEERING Stops...

I cruised along, and then suddenly, my mouth hit the floor of my car. My heart skipped. There he was—Tony Sparks—one of the most remarkable basketball specimens to ever come out of the gyms of Kansas City Central High School.

When I saw him, my heart froze in midstream. There he was hanging on the corner. It was as if I was watching a slow-motion picture. I could read his lips, and observe his mannerisms that spoke to me like an amplified loudspeaker.

There he was, staggering at the corner liquor store with a "fifth of wild Irish rose." He was flanked by his "ride or die" partners. Yes, the very same ones he hung out with in high school. The difference was, they looked like they belonged on the corner, and he seemed to be out of place trying to fit in. As I glared out my window, Tony still had the height, size, and physique, but it was apparent something had left him. You see, somewhere along the way, he had taken a detour from life's promising athletic script.

He did not achieve superstar status, like many talented people. He hit career-ending walls of adversity. But instead of pressing forward to break through its gravitational pull, he settled for becoming a legend in his own mind, a "casualty of war." He had all the promise and ability but was trapped in his own personal twilight zone, unable to pull out.

As Bishop T. D. Jakes has often stated, ***"Your gift can only carry you as far as your character can keep you."***

When the Cheering Stops and an athlete can't move on, sometimes he tends to spend a lot of time around the people that affirm him and feed his ego with "what used to be" or "should have been." He listens to them talk about the last-second shots, the girls in the stands, the parties, and the roar of the crowd. It takes great surrender to let go of the past and walk into the future.

Years ago there was a famous television show called the Twilight Zone. It would open with a character who had a problem or situation. Its creator, Rod Sterling, used to step into the scene before the very first act and begin to dialogue about the action that was about to take place, leaving the audience questioning the possibility of its outcome.

Unfortunately, there is no Rod Sterling to narrate this story. This story is about a real person with a real dilemma. Someone who was a "big baller" who had all the potential and promise, but through habits, association, or personal weaknesses, gets trapped in a life of what could have been versus a life of going forward with accomplishment and purpose.

When The CHEERING Stops...

I'm certainly not suggesting that to be considered successful in sports you have to be the superstar. But let's be honest, it is much harder for successful athletes to prepare to end their careers gracefully.

Another example is Reggie. He had become a shadow of the person he was previously. His body, once likened to that of a Greek Adonis, had deteriorated through several years of self-destruction and abuse. He self-medicated his pain through alcohol and drugs.

He couldn't seem to get it back together because he couldn't face his demons or forgive himself. But now, emotionally and mentally, he is not the menacing player that once terrorized his opponents.

Do you know a Reggie, an athlete incarcerated to the glories of his past, frustrated and unfulfilled? Yet, they must have the continued fix of hearing cheers, seeing or talking about how great they were and how they should have made it bigger.

When The CHEERING Stops...

During my sports career, and even in today's 24/7 sports media, I have found that the more incredible your athletic abilities and accomplishments, the harder it is to lay them down when the time comes to do so.

"We don't struggle with the ghost of our former self when we are submitted to where God wants to take our lives. It may hurt arriving there, but your true destiny is on the other side of what you're going through!"

Kenny Randle

It has been said that separation or divorce between two spouses is similar to "a death." It almost always bears with it various forms of pain, heartache, anger, and strife while going through the process of separating or severing the deteriorating relationship.

Sports is similar to marriage because of the love, commitment, and sacrifice you have made for the relationship. What's different in this relationship is you know entering into it that this sports marriage can have a short life span. So often, it is just one step away from separation.

One of the most challenging things for a highly committed and accomplished athlete who has experienced a deep love affair with their sport is to learn how to separate without going through the finality of a divorce. Although you are no longer playing at that high level, you can learn to enjoy it as a fan while transitioning to your next level in life.

I recall the day I finally came to grips with my future of no more training camps or trying to make the final roster. The dream of a long-term professional sports career path was not in the cards for me. It was time to stop chasing the brass ring and chart my course for new horizons.

I had to take a hard look inward at my other talents, skills, and attributes. I understood that they had to be honed and contoured for the challenges and opportunities ahead of me. Although I had accomplished a lifelong dream, I realized that there indeed was so much more ahead of me. The epitome of loss would be to stay stuck in an area that had already run its course.

Many years ago, I roomed with an athlete that sleepwalked. I'll never forget the day he told me. I recall saying to myself, "All I know is, he better stay on the other side of the room. And he better not come near me."

Amazingly enough, he told me that he was harmless and had never done anything freaky. Furthermore, he stated that if he ever sleepwalked, don't wake him up.

I shared that because many current and former athletes that are chronic sleepwalkers. They want to remain asleep to an unavoidable reality. They want to keep a false narrative alive. You see, sleepwalkers can walk, talk, and perform other motor skills while asleep. They look like they're functioning but really are asleep.

Someone needs to tell them what I was afraid to tell my roommate, "WAKE UP!" They're not focused on the truth of where they are or want to go. Those that sleepwalk through life's situations miss opportunities, direction, and the many blessings being "woke" offers.

I spent most of my USC college summers in Los Angeles, but at the end of my junior year, my homeboy and teammate Eric Williams met me in Provo, Utah, to watch me compete. I was confident that I had an excellent chance to win the 400-meter championships as a junior, and our team would smash the (still existing) world record for the 4x100 yard relay set by my alma mater.

Benny Brown of UCLA was ranked number one in the world by Track and Field News the year before. I was fortunate to have beat him twice within two weeks and felt good about my chances to do the same in Provo, Utah.

I was well on my way to realizing victory, but I didn't take care of myself. My resistance got low, and I got sick, causing my lymph nodes to swell up right before the championships at 4,549 feet above sea level. In that condition, I would be no match against world-class competition.

The championships were a bitter-sweet ending for me that year. After running the fastest time in the world for the 400 meters and being the favorite to win, I lost a race I should have dominated easily.

We drove back home in his always-reliable orange Volkswagen Beetle. Eric "Red" Williams was the best person in the world to travel alongside. He always kept conversation popping and was an excellent driver. So there we were, two wild, risk-taking, exploring, and simply crazy student-athletes taking a road trip to Kansas City. It was so cool for him to come. What a memorable moment!

When The CHEERING Stops...

I attended the 2004 NCAA Track & Field Championships in Austin, Texas a few years later. This is the crème de la crème, the best track and field athletes on the college level and the world.

I scheduled myself to be in Austin on business and attended every evening session of the competition. Upon arriving at the airport, I ran into a former Olympian turned sportscaster for track and field. Immediately, I began to recount the period when I had last seen him, which happened to be at these same championships. It felt good that someone would recognize me after all these years. He had been a world-class high jumper, and I had been a world-class quarter-miler. We both had dominated at the championships that year.

Well, that evening, the qualifying rounds began. No sooner had I taken my seat at the stadium, I was recognized by a few old-timers who fanatically follow the sport. They gave me glad handshakes, shared all the stats on my career, and caught me up on all the other old-timers I had not seen in many a year. I truly enjoyed the track meet. It could bring me back, remembering that I had competed and had great success at this level.

Then it began. During the final two days of the competition, I found myself drawn to the meets and reliving how it was so many years ago to compete and win at this level. I couldn't help but think about my glorious memories and the sense of accomplishment I was fortunate to achieve in this competitive sport.

Why do we desire to grab the brass ring just one more time? We see former world heavyweight boxers, well past their prime, attempt to regain the magic that once electrified their fans. They step once more into the ring, only to be plummeted by an opponent they could have easily beaten in their prime.

As athletes, we spend our lives competing with opponents and sacrificing our bodies with a deep and committed desire to be the best.

Indeed, as with any sports career, we have the commonality of draping ourselves with our athletic uniform and pageantry. But once it's over, we must begin putting on the uniforms of the new life, placing the old ones away.

Everyone touts that you must have money to have a significant impact. Let me be the first to tell you that money is an essential asset to have in your possession, but it's your mind or wisdom attached to the money that makes the difference.

I have found that athletes who have not incorporated, pursued, or developed the knowledge to position themselves for the next move, are subject to disappointment and failure.

When The CHEERING Stops...

Remember, "people failing to plan (invest) are people who are planning to fail." Most people don't leave their sports careers saying to themselves, "Man, I can't wait to fail, as I go forward!"

No, we never go forward to fail. It's not in our sports DNA. But if we never invest the time to apply ourselves to get educated both in and out of the sport, gaining more knowledge, cultivating a trade, or developing a small business, we will soon fail.

Likewise, if we are unwilling to begin learning from someone in business who has gone before us, walked through the minefields of life, we similarly are planning to fail. And we will stand at a disadvantage when it comes to the opportunity to be productive or successful.

Remember the old saying, *"If you're going to walk through a minefield, follow somebody."*

Reaching for past glory is a non-profitable use of our mental energy and time. A far better service would be to explore new areas or avenues of passion or interest. This will improve your likelihood of success.

When The CHEERING Stops...

Living In a Haunted House

One Thursday morning a friend and colleague rushed into my office, his eyes fixed on me, with heart racing and tiny beads of sweat dripping from his pale white forehead, and said,

"Kenny, Kenny," as he pushed his words out with difficulty and hyperventilated-induced stuttering, "I've not been able to sleep for two nights. I have to share something very personal with you. I recently went to see a psychiatrist to get help for a lot of recurring personal issues I've been living with for years, and after listening to me for a while, he said, "Do you know what your problem is? You're living in a haunted house!"

Little did Will know that this jolting statement shook me down to my very core. I couldn't help but conjure up all sorts of visions of my first trip to Disneyland's Haunted Mansion. There you are escorted through a mock haunted house equipped with ghostly ghouls and apparitions running loose throughout the mansion, screeching and laughing loudly out of control.

I imagined them chasing him through every corridor of the house and giving him no possible peace. Every door of escape was locked. But unfortunately, he never awakened to realize this was no dream but his reality.

When The CHEERING Stops...

Honestly, I don't subscribe to the notion of ghosts spending eternity haunting the souls of men. But we tend to allow ourselves to be haunted by what should have been or could have been. "If only I could have kept playing and had three more years, or coach liked me. I would have accomplished so much." We're haunted by things that occurred deep in our past. We're haunted by broken promises, unfulfilled dreams, and missed moments.

I too, had my moments in a haunted house, unsure of where reality ended and fiction began. It seemed to be a thin line between hanging on to *what was* and stopping my failures and unattained goals from haunting and keeping me from the future God had for me.

Do you know the scariest thing I have witnessed and experienced as a world-class athlete? Dealing with the "*what could have beens.*"

"If only I hadn't torn the knee. If only the doctor hadn't botched the surgery. If only I got a fair shake to make the team."

I've carried these around like I was wearing a cheap suit.

Now, in many cases, there are reasons that have some validity. But, unfortunately, most people don't pay you or celebrate you for what you could have been, only for what you do now. If you're going to live in this world successfully, you have to come to grips with the fact that it's one of subjectivity. This means people have the prerogative or personal choice to accept or reject you. You don't have a lot of say in the matter other than allowing your talent and attitude to do the talking for you.

The book of Proverbs says **that "A gift opens the way and ushers the giver into the presence of the great." (Proverbs 18:16, NIV)**

I am either a victim of circumstances or a victor over my predicaments. You must break away from the victimizing voices, even if they are your own. I know because I successfully pushed myself to run out the door of that haunted house, and never go back in again.

When the cheering stops, many athletes are left in a haunted house state of mind. Like in the movies, they feel that there is no way out. As a result, they are constantly tormented by missed opportunities, uncaptured moments, mistakes, and deals gone badly.

It may seem like a simple task to chalk up your past athletic experiences and relationships as great experiences and memories and move on down the road. But when your past haunts you, it takes more than a pep talk to move forward even the most successful.

When The CHEERING Stops...

We will always be haunted in our minds by images, experiences, and spirits if we fail to take authority and control over those things that attempt to overtake and dominate our thoughts and actions.

I have found this to be the difference between the athletes that move on in the afterlife of sports and those who tour the haunted house.

We all have to reconcile with our past. Sometimes, the constant effort of sweeping our past under the rug builds up such a huge lump in the carpet that we or others eventually trip over it. At that point, we only have a couple of options. Either we continue to act as if there is no issue, which most of us athletes were raised and mentored to do. Or, we work through the pain, get back up, and go again. The ultimate truth is sometimes we may need help or assistance, and guess what? It's okay to ask for it.

So, how does one deal with past failures, mistakes, or missed opportunities? First, look for the things inside of you that give you the grit and graciousness to continue moving forward. It's not the big stumbling blocks that usually derail us. It's the small ones anchored in our past that cause us to repeat.

When The CHEERING Stops...

Part 3: The Pedestals We Build

The Pedestals We Build

From Pee-Wee to Gladiators

Gladiator fights began in Rome around 245 AD. Men and women traveled near and far to celebrate and cheer heroes as they fought and competed for fame, glory, and legendary status. They were lifted on pedestals and viewed as if they were gods!

Athletes in the 21st century are the modern gladiators. Their legendary status fills up our stadiums and arenas with thousands of idolizing and dedicated fans heaping praise and adoration at a level that makes them seem bigger than life.

Columnist Richard Clark wrote that *"sports is only a microcosm of our society."* I agree that we have developed sports addictions and become athlete worshippers in America. If you want to get an upfront and personal look at a country or nation's DNA, just look at its sports teams: violent, disruptive, self-consumed, and all packaged within a "win at all cost culture."

Even though my competitive years in sports have long since passed, winning and competing is still one of the ultimate highs. The truth of the matter is the endorphins of winning never leave you as an athlete. You were trained to compete and win, so naturally, it becomes a part of your DNA. There are only a few things in life that compare to the thrill of winning a game, a series, or a major championship. It is a high like no other and it is very hard to come down from without longing for more.

Clark went on to write that *"we like to pretend that sports represent the best of life or a person."*

It's undeniably true that sports represent and present valuable life lessons. But it's the "best" part that you can leave off that statement. It does not represent the best of life or a person, but it does represent an aspect of one's life that can be very rewarding in the life lessons it produces.

As Clark goes on to explain, *"Sports is an exact microcosm of society. It dramatizes and emulates the real world today, with its violence, greed, selfishness, corruption, and entitlement."* All are found today in the sports world.

Even the TMZs of the world got into the act because just like sex sells in magazines, sports may sell more because of its appeal. People worldwide will pay to be entertained, and the convergence of sports marketing, corporate sponsors, and the exponential levels of money it attracts allows any viewing audience to get hooked watching it 24 hours a day.

I'm always careful not to throw stones at glasshouses. But, if slinging a few rocks at today's multi-billion-dollar-driven industry can grab someone's attention, then here comes my rock! So duck, you win-at-all-costs coaches, overbearing out-of-control parents, social-promoting teachers, and above-the-law athletes.

It was the autopsy of the legendary center for the Pittsburgh Steelers, Mike Webster that lifted the veil of ignorance and exposed the NFL to what it had been denying and sweeping under the rug. All the while discrediting any non-NFL connected doctor that would dare bring the negative findings forward.

Most players, both old and current, along with their family and friends, not only appreciated (NFL owners excluded) but were shocked at the findings of Dr. Bennet Omalu when he discovered a new disease by the name of chronic traumatic encephalopathy or CTE.

The NFL had done its best to use the defense "the brutality and violence of the sport come with the territory," and "players knew what they were getting into when they signed up." Still, the sport had created a multi-billion dollar entertainment industry. It kept the billion-dollar machine cranking by explaining away or discrediting medical findings. However, they couldn't hide the long-term effects and life-threatening health problems surrounding concussion injuries of NFL players.

I understand what sports truly means and while it is an excellent part of our culture, it is but a microcosm of life. There is so much more on the menu for you, just like I told my Brother in Law.

Pee-Wee Sports or Gladiator Complex

Pee-Wee sports begin when you're old enough to put on oversized baggy uniforms and helmets too big for your head resembling the novelty "bobblehead dolls" on the dashboards of cars back in the '60s.

At a very young age you are put into a process of mental, physical, and emotional conditioning that, over time, becomes ingrained in your heart, mind, and athletic psyche. I've come to call it the "Gladiator Complex." This complex causes a player to take on a mindset that you must persevere no matter how bad the injury. So, unless you are physically unable to walk or be carried out on a stretcher, you "get your butt back on the field or court and play" for fear of someone else taking your spot. Sometimes this is done for fear of being seen as too soft.

When The CHEERING Stops...

You see, playing hurt in any sport, whether contact or non-contact, comes with the territory and becomes part of the DNA of an athlete.

An old saying states, "The cream always rises to the top." As an athlete it means that in almost every contest, important event, or moment, the very best can call on something deep down within and perform!

They are the ones that seem to thrive on these kinds of moments which can make the game slow down and come to them. All the time realizing they must put it all on the line, even if it means placing the team on their back to show their resolve, toughness, and leadership. Usually, this is done to inspire or ignite their team, the coaches, and adoring fans, to defeat their opponent.

I suppose it's like being a gladiator apprentice entering gladiator school. You are taught and raised along with your peers that daily compete with you not to hurt, not to cry, but to suck it up. You must be on point every play, every moment, and by any means necessary.

This is taught to the American athlete from childhood. It's what fills the stands, sells jerseys, creates heroes, and promotes the hero-worship status of athletes in our culture.

When The CHEERING Stops...

As a young athlete, it's healthy to have athletic heroes that you look up to and admire. That level of admiration can drive and push us to emulate them and their results. But make sure our Pee-Wee gladiators develop character traits that prevent the "Gladiator Complex."

One essential element we must not forget is the component of "character." Strong character must wholeheartedly be injected to help develop the young athlete's sense of worth. Unfortunately, all too often, in today's society, we're willing to sacrifice positive character and integrity for the prospect of gaining stardom and notoriety.

Sports marketing in America has reached a major pinnacle in the business of sports. It has birthed mega-million dollar contracts, product endorsements, more contracts, and other great opportunities for athletes.

There is a message somewhat lost that once was a loud roar in this country. That was the message of "Just saying No!" Saying no to performance-enhancing drugs or even to drugs that have become acceptable by the culture. Yet what does this message or mixed message say to our youth and young male and female athletes?

When The CHEERING Stops...

Sometimes we quickly escort our kids out of the classroom, not proficient in reading or writing. Yet they are encouraged or enticed to envision multi-million dollar shoe contracts! How can you blame them? The messages bombard them constantly and intentionally by planting influencers to make their interests known to upcoming superstars even as early as middle school.

I recall going to the local middle school to work out and seeing coaches working out young children like college athletes. In all too many cases, the parents were sitting on the sidelines in lawn chairs, cheering the process. Something about that challenged my thinking about whether we are so focused on a big payday that we are willing to interrupt childhood innocence for the possibility of a big payday.

Everyone desires some form or level of recognition. Even workers in a manufacturing plant, on the floor of an assembly line, when the team has produced more widgets with fewer accidents, and your picture is posted in the employee breakroom for everyone to see, that recognition feels great.

Yet when it comes to recognition, some crave it as an addict craves drugs so much that they would do anything for it. Whether the recognition comes through family, adoring fans, groupies, or colleagues. There is nothing greater than the coach saying, "You had a phenomenal game tonight, one of your very best," recognition is addicting for an athlete.

There is an innate desire in every human being to be recognized, whether by peers, families, or co-workers. Imagine the accolades from adoring fans, media, and even opponents when you score a buzzer beater or set a world record. It is the epitome of recognition.

That reminds me of the time the Cleveland Browns drafted me. I was straight out of college heading to spring camp, and there was a mixer of veteran players and rookies wanting to make an impression. When I and a few others arrived at the airport, two women met us. These were not college types, either. They wanted to know who we were, when we were drafted, and anything we needed because they could make it happen for us.

I think you may guess where I'm going. Well nothing happened, so let your imagination snap back! Oh, we thought we were a big deal until we told veteran players who met us at the airport, and they called them by name and described what they looked like. It was hilarious! You see, all "ballers" thrive on recognition because it gives us the attention we crave.

When The CHEERING Stops...

In many ways, athletes take on the form of modern-day gladiators sent out to embrace the sounds of voices, horns, horses, and haters awaiting them in the coliseum.

While recognition is addicting to an athlete, combining it with reward, now that's next level! Who doesn't want their effort and hard work to be rewarded? We learned this pattern as kids when our parents, teachers, or instructors awarded us for singing well, spelling well, getting an A on a quiz or exam, or maybe something as simple as raking all the leaves from the yard.

Competing, winning, accomplishing, and receiving rewards for your efforts are great motivators. In addition, an athlete wants to receive immediate feedback. In pro football, there's an old saying that says "you're only as good as your next play."

Tell me if you recall something similar to this *"Good play and good effort, Kevin. Keep that up and stay committed to working hard, and you can be a Starter one day."*

Can we all admit there is absolutely nothing wrong with receiving rewards? Kevin just wanted to be the best he could be and have a coach who believed in him. So the coach dangled the carrot of accomplishment and reward to push him further and make him work harder. The carrot of accomplishment is very powerful.

To both the past and present-day athletes, the rewards of their sport have always proceeded with accomplishment. Although it's often just getting to the top of the mountain to prove and let others know you could do it. But, for many, the reward is the association, the fraternity, or team camaraderie over the seasons and years.

After the Cheering Stops, many athletes find themselves looking for situations, careers, or positions with that team element of recognition and reward. Yet, for some, the fulfillment is never replicated. I spoke to one of my "besties" that played in the NFL for eight seasons, and he told me it took him a year and a half before he even knew what to do next.

Sometimes players love the game and the roar of the crowd or winning so much they are willing to risk it all by taking performance-enhancing drugs or nootropics, beta-blockers, or whatever it takes to win.

A famous quote has been misquoted through the years by Legendary NFL Hall of Fame Football Coach Vince Lombardi. He's quoted as saying, **"Winning isn't everything. It's the**

only thing." But he actually said *"**Winning isn't everything, but wanting to win is.**"*

We are a society obsessed with winning, but we get it honestly. The Bible tells us that God said to take dominion over the Earth and subdue it! Gen. 1:28. Now, if that's not competitive, what is? The Almighty God of the Universe created us to win. But those that succeed in today's world sometimes forsake sportsmanship and the integrity of the game.

We all need to be recognized and rewarded for things we have done well. The truth is the people we desire it from are the people we love and admire the most. Athletes care about those close to them.

Recognition goes deep into the heart of young athletes. Simple statements from coaches like, "You are the best young athlete to ever come out of this area, and you can be a real champion one day." This level of conversation, sowed in a young athlete's heart, can leave an indelible impression in their life. Especially if there is no real father figure or stable parents in the home to love, encourage, instruct, and instill visions of hope towards life's many challenges.

"Johnny, you are some kind of athlete! You are one of the most gifted running backs this state has ever seen come down the pike in all my years of coaching. Son, all that matters is that you keep runnin' that ball as you do. Stay focused, and don't worry about anything else. You'll have it made!"

What Coach didn't share with Johnny was the other side of talent, which involves real consequences and real-life requirements that life sometimes throws your way. Like injury, heartache, disappointment, and aspects of reality not registered in the playbook.

I know you think our boys are too young to hear these kinds of messages. You might think, "It's too soon to talk about how consequences could hinder their passion. It might make them timid and hurt their fearless nature!"

But let me ask you, have you ever heard some of the messages this new breed Pee-Wee & Pop Warner coaches shout at their players? So, then they are not too young to hear about the consequences.

The reality is that coaches on all levels play an important part in the life of an athlete, but what we teach and instill in them at their youngest and most impressionable ages has a lasting impact. However, today's sports culture requires us to temper and balance that messaging with the realities of what they grow up and experience!

When The CHEERING Stops...

Our kids must know that the money is not automatic. According to world-renown leadership expert John Maxwell, "Talent is never enough." Simply being an athlete doesn't equate to money.

There are a lot of tremendously gifted athletes in this world. Yet any coach worth their salt will tell you that there is always somebody BETTER. Even if they haven't arrived on the scene yet, they are only a few years away from showing up to challenge and exceed what you've done.

My young superstars, there is always someone out there greater, someone who will replace you when you are no longer valuable or cannot produce. They're just waiting for their opportunity.

Professional athletes have a short sports life. The average running back in the NFL only lasts 2.5 years, and many other sports have short lifespans. I'll be the first to agree that there are a few exceptions to the rule: Michael Jordan, LeBron James, Tom Brady, and Miguel Carera are just a few of them.

When The CHEERING Stops...

Athletes Desire Three Things:

* ♣ **Recognition**

* ♣ **Rewards**

* ♣ **Relationship**

It's an athlete's competitive drive or nature that pushes them to excellence, the desire to achieve greatness and reach higher heights of performance and accomplishment. But it's the "recognition factor" even after their sport is finished that burns like a laser cutting a permanent place in their emotional psyche.

Often when the career is over and the recognition is no longer there, many players will act out to generate attention even if it causes negative consequences. The craving for recognition is so compelling that it can also propel some players into very positive and worthwhile directions. This craving can cause them to achieve admiration and success in business or other areas of life.

We should never allow talent and outstanding athletic ability to replace character and integrity.

First, we must teach and remind our kids that those they reverence and admire as superstars are simply men and women with unique God-given talents and abilities. They have worked extremely hard to develop and cultivate that talent to show the world their greatness.

Four key roles influence our Pee-Wee gladiators and continue to do so throughout their lives: parents, teachers, coaches, and fans. To develop and cultivate character for a successful athletic career and life, parents shouldn't live their lives or athletic dreams at the expense of their kids.

Teachers, please don't look the other way regarding assignments, grading or behavior. They will need your high expectations to move forward and improve.

Coaches don't let winning at all costs cause personal character to take a back seat. You are significant to the process of shaping our young athletes. And finally, fans don't forget that athletes are humans. They cut, bleed, hurt, and make mistakes just like you.

It's a Matter of Life and Death:

(A familiar scenario)

"Jay, you're right, you have been invaluable to this team and taken us to multiple championships, but with the injury you sustained last year, well, your skills have diminished. The truth of the matter is that this sport is a young man's game, and. And we need someone younger to step in and become the future. I'm sorry. Unfortunately, you're just like the rest of us. We all reach that point in time when we have to 'let go of the game' and move on with our lives."

"Coach, I don't know how to let go. No one ever taught me how to do that or even prepare for it. This is the only thing I've ever known or ever wanted to do."

Two Weeks Later

"Order in this court. I'll have order in this court!" shouted the petite yet fiery Judge Shammis as she carefully peered from her bench and assayed the media landscape, which had turned her courtroom into a circus for the past three months.

"I want the family, friends, media, and everyone else to be seated. Reporters, no tape recorders or flash cameras

allowed. If you do, I'll have you removed from my courtroom immediately, never to return."

Jay Barry Swift was the league's most valuable player. He was "off the charts athletically gifted," yet one of the most controversial wide-receivers to ever grace the field.

His physical attributes were legendary. He ran an unheard of 4.3 forty-yard dash, at 6'5", 235 lbs. and a vertical leap of 45". This made him athletically freakish, to say the least. However, the many scouts who witnessed him play in college said he effortlessly did astounding leaps, acrobatic play, and record-breaking runs. It was as though he still had another gear left when needed. No one doubted that he would be unstoppable as an NFL Pro.

"Everything these past several days has been grossly exaggerated! No truth whatsoever!" screamed Jay Barry while on the witness stand. "I'm being set up, and by who, I don't know, but when I find him...."

The problems started when Jay Barry began to decline physically. He could no longer leap over defensive backs or break through the arm tackles of some of the league's strongest and hardest-hitting safeties.

When The CHEERING Stops...

The federal court almost concluded its final day of questioning, and testimonies brought evidence that the player was a participant and partnered in a performance-enhancing drug operation. He was accused of selling and distributing the products throughout the league and across other sports, baseball, basketball, and track.

You see, Jay Barry had also rewritten all the league's receiving records. As a result, handsomely received a blockbuster contract of $12 million a year, not including TV endorsements and personal appearances that accounted for another $15 million.

In the backdrop of his life, he had taken to drugs to maintain his physicality and speed. The only problem was the toll it had taken on the once-storied athlete. Instead of shredding and victimizing defenses, he had become the victim.

The last eight days were filled with lengthy testimonies from friends, relatives, coaches, and other players called as character witnesses for Jay Barry in hopes of redeeming him in the eyes of the court. Finally, it was Jay Barry's turn to come forward and speak.

"Mr. Swift," the judge stated, "I believe the court understands clearly from your testimony that your drug addiction problem and subsequent drug trafficking indictment

took place while you were still out on the field making millions of dollars playing football with thousands of young cheering fans, week after week, on TV sets all over the country.

Yet, you blew it all for a carload full of drugs!" The judge paused for a moment and then continued. "The testimonies show that you also had a brush in high school with drugs but you were released on your own recognizance to the hands of your high school coach, promising never to return to this pattern again!

Mr. Swift, it appears that no one cared enough about you to tell you that the lifestyle you chose to embrace was going to lead you into trouble when you needed to hear it. Now you have to look a judge like me in the face, and I have to be the one addressing it and hopefully get you the help you need.

Now, we, the U.S. Government, must do what the league or your college coaches should have done years before now. The jury of your peers finds you guilty with suspension from the league for life, and you will do some prison time!"

In an instant, that arrogant "you can't touch me" attitude began to unravel and was replaced with panic.

"You don't understand. A lot of athletes do it. I had to do it. I had to compete to be the best, stay strong, and keep up. I

just couldn't end it. I had to hold on in any way possible. It can't end like this, not like this!"

"Above the Law"

Here's another example that we have heard far too many times over the years. According to the statement, the police told the alleged victim to "think long and hard" and that her life could be made miserable if she proceeded with the case against Winston.

The Tallahassee Democrat reported that the case had been put on hold because the accuser stopped cooperating but was now reopened because of new information.

"But Mike, the girl said that you slapped, beat and hit her full-fisted. Go right now, apologize, and get it right before she presses charges, kills your career, and embarrasses this university. We have a reputation to uphold!"

"Coach, I didn't mean to do it, but she pushed my button and made me mad. I told her that I was under a lot of pressure with school and football. There's a lot of stuff on my head! But she didn't care, she just kept getting in my face, and I don't take

that from no woman! She should be honored just to have somebody like me. Do you know how many women would line up to be in her place?

But Coach, I need your help on this, man. It won't happen again. Can you get me out of it just this last time? And I promise I won't go this way again. We got to win this thing on Friday night!"

"Mike," the coach sighed deeply, "let me see what I can do, but I think it's too late."

Basically, Mike is saying, "I'm too proud and full of myself to take ownership of what I did. So now please wave a magic wand and get me out of this mess!"

We all know that there is no reasonable defense for Mike's actions. Still, unfortunately, too many of our touted and celebrated athletes blame it on everyone and everything other than themselves! They expect coaches to bail them out, which has become increasingly difficult in this social media era.

Therefore, it's absolutely essential to teach our Pee Wee gladiators values and responsibility to prevent things like this from ever happening.

When The CHEERING Stops...

Look at the real-life events of the last several years. Star players caught on camera doing inappropriate and morally repugnant things. Careers have been ruined and lives crushed, so the league has been forced to reckon with this behavior.

While it is not indicative of every coach or player, it happens all too often. This type of behavior must be dealt with starting at the high school level and earlier by teaching values, responsibility, and consequences. Otherwise, it becomes acceptable, causing problems at subsequent levels and damaging so many lives and careers.

"Robert, so glad you could meet with us here at the station on Prime Time Sports to discuss the outstanding effort you had against the New York Titans last week. But we also understand that a fan accused you of hurling insults and profanity at him in front of his kids. He was persistent in wanting a picture and you signing his basketball. Do you think your behavior was indicative of the image you want to project to young aspiring athletes?"

"Hear me loud and clear. I never signed up to be anyone's Role Model."

That's probably the most significant difference between today's modern athletes and the athletes of old. So many today are shying away from being called a role model. I suppose it's because the badge of honor has become a weight of responsibility much heavier than anticipated.

Today's athletes can't even blink or smile the wrong way before it's all over ESPN, CNN, or TMZ. Especially when reporters try to find any story or angle, while the player has to find a way out without getting caught up. But an athlete needs to develop character and find the proper tools to navigate through adverse circumstances that arise, including the media.

A monster has been created in today's multi-billion dollar, high-profile win-at-all-costs sports world. It's not a singular occurrence or mutation in our society, but a mass production bred from our high school, middle school, and college sports factories. I call it the "Frankenstein Factor."

Over the past 20 years, with the advent of cable and sports networks, there has been an amazing acceleration of multi-million dollar sports contracts and endorsements. As a result, athletes earn millions as commercial pitch people for athletic shoes, clothing, cars, energy drinks, soft drinks and fast foods!

Whether college or professional, the scrutiny of high-profile athletes has hit an all-time high. Today, the American Athlete is surrounded by media scrutiny and the ever-increasing social media outlets that speak both for and against the sports world. These places have become great job and career opportunities for athletes leaving their time on the field or court. Today our American society is transfixed with sports and winning. Nothing wrong with that, but at all costs? Think about it!

When The CHEERING Stops...

Part 4: Making the Transition

Making the Tranistion

It All Begins with Self-Discipline

There were times in my life when I had to determine where I was going and what I was to do even as I continued to set goals. I continued to seek God, praying and believing that things would change. Then I surrendered myself to the process of getting around those that could help me.

Making a decision alone is not always the best answer. At times you may have gotten off the highway at the wrong exit. You may need to engage with someone that can help you get back on the best road to continue your journey. That navigator maybe someone you can show your map to and say, "listen I'm looking at this map, but I'm not quite sure of the coordinates of where I need to go. Should I go east or do I need to go west?" Allow someone else to be your personal GPS along with your faith in God.

"On Christ the solid rock I stand, all other ground is sinking sand" was the chorus that rang out so as I sat there as a fidgeting little boy upon the long church pews at Rosser Simpson

When The CHEERING Stops...

C.M.E. Church. While that song had much meaning from a spiritual standpoint, it also adds truth as we look and see the many athletes around us who have mortgaged their future careers and opportunities by building their houses on shaky ground.

It was the Pro-Football off-season in my rookie year, a time when most rookies would migrate back to their respective college campus to work out or hang out with other pros or former teammates from college. Many purchased homes, condos or looked for apartments in the off-season to show others they were making it happen for themselves.

Many athletes can personally find themselves on shaky and vulnerable ground, even with all the privileges and visible trappings of notoriety, accomplishment, and success. For it's hard to accept the fact that if we build a great house on a poor foundation, it has the possibility of crumbling and deteriorating

For example, when I bought my first house, it was wonderful. I was excited and anxious about getting in that house and finally enjoying it with my new bride. Yet I recall during the walkthrough and before signing the final paperwork, I observed cracks in the wall and ceiling. I paused because I thought there was an issue and we might have problems later on. The salesperson was a burly Texan with an intimidating voice and seemed to be rushing me to close the sale. He was anxious to have me sign.

I remember stopping everything in the middle of the week and asking, "John, let me ask you a question. Who's buying this house? You or me?"

He answered, "You," as if irritated with me for asking.

"That's what I thought," I replied, "so let's slow this down and examine this house for my peace of mind."

That's what we need to do in life, slow things down so we can see the whole landscape. Athletes should begin this process by getting perspective from mentors or trusted advisors. We need to be careful not to be so anxious to get to the end game that we don't observe the cracks in our slab or insecure foundation. What cracks in your slab need addressing? Maybe it's time to swallow your pride and ask someone you genuinely trust for some advice or direction.

The next step in the process of slowing things down is building a solid foundation infused with integrity, character, and discipline. It follows the same patterns that we're taught in sports. It's prudent to take the time to repair any cracks in our private foundation. That's why mentors (teachers, coaches, parents, advisors, etc.) are so valuable. They see the things we cannot or refuse to see.

During that pro football off-season, my former college roommate and I looked at homes. Actually, he was the one looking because I was too broke to pay attention. Gary was the third overall pick in the NFL draft the year before, while I was drafted in the 7th round. He made the New York Giants, while I got cut from the Cleveland Browns in the next to last pre-season football game against the Minnesota Vikings. I was going with him to offer some color commentating during the drive.

Gary was one of those personalities that you either loved or hated. I hosted him on his first recruiting trip to USC before he signed his letter of intent. He was 6'5 and 270 lbs. with a 32-inch waist and looked like someone had taken a chisel and carved him out of solid marble!

Some players had an issue with Gary's abrasive personality off the field. He was confident and intimidating and always reminded us that he was the "woman's pet and every man's threat." For some reason, he and I had a mutual admiration because we both respected what we each had accomplished in our main sports. Although I was a good football player at USC, Gary was a great one!

When The CHEERING Stops...

He was first-team All-American, and I was a consensus Track and Field All-American. So these were pretty notable accomplishments from two out-of-state kids making it big at a perennial sports powerhouse like the University of Southern California.

While driving towards a very exclusive area outside of Los Angeles, we came upon one of the most gorgeous homes I had ever seen. It was a beautiful custom Spanish-style home that sat on a hill overlooking a valley with cattle grazing at the bottom. As I stepped towards the back of the house and looked out of the sliding glass doors, it hit me that one day this house could slide right off the back of this hill due to soil erosion.

Our lives can mimic that too. In the weeks leading up to the house-hunting venture, Southern California was bombarded with ongoing rains. As we entered the house and walked inside, what immediately caught my eye was the costly Spanish in-laid tiles throughout the entire house. It was a custom-made home with every amenity you could dream of or imagine. It was the type of place that would take your breath away at every angle.

We liked hanging out together because we both appreciated the finer things the world had to offer. You see, Gary had a lot of money now, and he wanted to experience life's best available to him. We had similar visions about exploring and experiencing the finer aspects of life. He had the provision to do so, and I just had the vision at the time. I greatly admired Gary because he was one of those rare breeds of athletes always trying to be around business and connect with people who could teach him.

When you are young, of course, you want to have fun and enjoy life. Our group of athletes had immense fun, and we were definitely CRAZY, but we were the best of the best. We were coached well, parented well, and appreciated the great opportunities.

Webster defines Self-Discipline as: *The ability to control one's feelings and overcome one's weaknesses; the ability to pursue what one thinks is right despite temptations to abandon it.*

Self-discipline is one of the most critical traits in the heart of all great champions. However, when we hear the words *self-discipline* and athletics most think they are Siamese twins. They go together like peanut butter and jelly, but that's simply not true. I've been around many talented athletes throughout my sports career with high-level skills but exhibited low discipline. This ultimately becomes the catalyst for their demise.

When The CHEERING Stops...

Some of you may know a person who is so talented that if you opened Webster's dictionary their picture would be shown in the definition. I'm talking about the guy who could throw the football 65 yards on a dime and hit the receiver in full stride. Yet he didn't learn the required discipline to run the plays sent into the game by the coach.

I'm reminded of someone who routinely ignored the coach's plays and often shot from half-court. As a result, he ended up flunking out of a JC and was involved in a convenience store robbery. Nothing else has been heard of him, but he represents all too many awesomely talented players with poor or no discipline.

Before there were three-pointers, this Phenom would shoot from almost half-court as comfortably as most could shoot from the free-throw line. We all have our playground sports stories that are probably under scrutiny and are more myth than reality. But one thing was real, this Phenom couldn't or wouldn't be coached and had no self-discipline.

Self-discipline is something developed inside of you. That's why it's called "self-discipline" because you create it.

Self-discipline is the ultimate *teacher-pupil* relationship. Just like when Jesus Christ walked this Earth and made the statement, "unless a grain of wheat falls to the ground and dies, it cannot live." That demand is to die to yourself so that you may live.

Take Tiger Woods. No one would dare argue his legendary trait of self-discipline. My experience has shown that this applies to anyone who dares to be the greatest in their field. It applies to the top CEO, the most graceful ballerina, and the actor dedicated to their craft. They know that being the best takes diligence and an unwavering commitment to excellence.

That includes a strong will and desire. It's irrelevant that you have to get up at 4:00 am to begin your training regiment, knowing that your muscles are screaming at you from the previous day's workout. Your mind is whispering, "You need to stay in bed this time and get more sleep." But, the will to be the best and live your passion and dreams causes you to get up and do it another time.

Do not confuse the term self-discipline with natural giftedness. This world has many mega-talented athletes. Though they may be great, some lack that one significant trait, discipline. Instead, they opt to live off their ability and talent alone, never reaching their full potential. I bet that if you could sit down and ask NFL greats like Emmitt Smith or Deon Sanders (a few of the best running backs in NFL history) to share the most important element of the game, they would say, "DISCIPLINE."

One of the most difficult transitions I had to accomplish in leaving the sports world was the transition into the business world. Many would say that's not a big transition because sports is a business. It's big business!

I'd say you're absolutely right, but the difference was I went from doing something I had reached a level of mastery in, both physically and mentally, to a world I knew little about, the world of business. Although I was around it because I worked for those who made it all work.

Not to say there's no mental aspect to sports. But generally, the people who have mastered their game in their head rise to the superstar level.

As athletes, we have been raised and wired to compete and perform from kindergarten to our professional lives. We take competition to heart and have to perform to prove ourselves. Unless you let that former self die, you can never live again. The divine ruler of the universe doesn't care about your performance. He is more interested in you being perfected in him.

We are performing for others our entire lives. Pleasing coaches, pleasing teachers, pleasing parents but never really pleasing ourselves. When we die to ourselves, we are trying to find ourselves. Too often, we are trying to get to the next level, when we should be getting ready for the next season. Doors are important because they make us want to knock to see what's on the other side.

It doesn't take a lot to get on an elevator and press a button to go up because everybody wants to go up. On the other hand, it takes more than just innate curiosity to knock on a door and find out what's behind it. It takes work. So maybe we should do more knocking, seeking, and asking.

It's time to Say Y.E.S. to your Future:

<u>Y</u>our <u>E</u>xit <u>S</u>trategy

You need to learn to say Y.E.S. to the transition beginning the next iteration of your life.

Y.E.S. stands for **Your Exit Strategy**. I took this radical approach to make these impactful steps manifest. This is a list of the Eight Essential Steps needed to begin the transition:

When The CHEERING Stops...

Eight Essential Steps to Exit with Excellence

1. Decide exactly what you want and what you're willing to give up to get what you want

2. Get around people that can help you get what you want

3. Set goals based on what you want

4. Plan your work and work your plan

5. Find mentors that have the expertise you need

6. Get the right mindset

7. Act like your trying out for a new sport

8. Stop hanging out with people still playing in the game, furthering their dreams when you should be about creating your next chapter.

1: Decide what you want and what you're willing to give up to get what you want.

Someway or somehow, you may have taken a detour off the map or gotten off course. If you've been off the course for some time it is hard to decide what you want because you don't know the direction. So the very first step is deciding what you want. Say Y.E.S. to your future by implementing Your Exit Strategy.

This can be the most difficult decision because of the disappointment or downward spiral you have repeatedly experienced. It could be as drastic as an addiction, injury, or medical condition that sidelined you and you don't know how to get on track. That's when step #2 comes in.

2: Get around the people who can help you get what you want

That's when the spirit of humility steps in, and you admit "I need some help and when asking for that help, share what you're willing to do as a part of the request for that help.

If there's anything I can stress or convey to you as an athlete reading this book, it would be to *"always develop and leverage your connections, both great and small."* These people who admire you, want to hang out, take pictures, go to dinner with you could be invaluable relationships one day.

Often athletes, don't manage relationships because they are too concerned about people wanting to get next to them, concerned they want something from them, versus who they are. In developing relationships, you need to look at it as you're not just making friends but building your digital phone book. You don't have to have them as close friends, but it's valuable to have them as good connections that could lead to great connections.

Through the years, I've learned that most people that care about you want to help if you ask. The world belongs to the askers, so ask for help!

3: Set goals based on what you want

Understand that the world does not revolve around you as an athlete, but it does revolve. So the question is how will you find yourself in the midst of all of it? First, you have to reach out to people close to you who will reach out to those close to them to help you find your next steps in discovering what you want.

4: Plan your Work and Work your Plan

There is nothing wrong with planning for your next move (at least on paper). What's your blueprint for the next two to five years? Ten years? What happens after retirement? *Plan your work and work your plan. The secret is work.*

"People failing to plan are people planning to fail." The only way to live after sports is to ***"plan the transition."*** This makes you unstoppable because no one can stop a man with a plan because no one has a plan to stop him! Be unstoppable!

5: Find mentors that have the expertise you need

People envy and admire your ability to utilize your contacts and relationships gained throughout your career simply because of what you could do. Many connected to you give others a feeling of sharing in your success circle.

So the message is simple. While you're connecting at alumni events, autograph sessions, leasing cars from dealers, and doing public appearances, pick their brains about becoming successful. It will help you visualize how you can one day own a dealership, embark on a broadcasting career, or any of a hundred different avenues you can pursue. The time is now!

6: Get the right mindset

Everyone wants to be associated with winners and greatness. An adage says, ***"There is no better time than the present,"*** and the present for the modern-day athlete is **NOW**. Shift your mindset to know there is more on the menu. Athletes are used to people reaching out for them and now must shift the mindset to reach out for people.

7: Act like your trying out for a new sport

During our lives as athletes, we are taught to perform, ***"Look at little Johnny, can't he really dance?"* "Listen to Jessica sing. Her voice is so amazing, sing Jessica."*** No matter who it's for, an athlete translates this as "***hey, look at me, notice me.***" As athletes, we need to use and apply that exact performance-oriented nature inbred in us through our sports career.

8: Stop hanging out with people still playing in the game, furthering their dreams, when you should be about creating your next chapter!

Often athletes will play intramural sports or hang out watching other athletes play, fulfilling their dreams. But, realize that doing so keeps you from pursuing and fulfilling your dreams and creating your next chapter. So, don't turn from being on the field of play to being a spectator.

Most athletes have spent many years building strong work ethics. In many cases, time, success, and exposure can assist those who have had challenging backgrounds to break free from all the ghosts of the past that can haunt or limit advancement.

Making the Transition

Today's world invokes mega-success dreams and mega-million dollar hopes of being on TV, having your own shoe brand, or being a great sport and business tycoon like LeBron James or Magic Johnson. But every forward-thinking athlete must do a steely-eyed reality check.

The truth of the matter is, it's far better to work to be successful in the area of your passion, and if that doesn't work exactly as planned, then find something else connected to your passion and pursue it for all that it's worth.

In my opinion, many athletes bog themselves down in their physical attributes and don't focus on honing their character, skills, and talents for life beyond sports.

Every athlete must face three difficulties to make the transition: adjusting their game, finding balance between the mental and the physical, and knowing how to release what's in them so they know where to start.

Adjusting the Game

Any athlete that has ever reached success has earned or created within themselves what today we call "swag," but I call it another name: *the Confidence Factor!*

This Confidence Factor resides deep within the athlete's psyche. It emanates from the body of results they have delivered on the field, court, or track, contest upon contest, competition after competition, in pressure cooker situations. It has forged unmatched confidence in their ability to compete and win.

This "Confidence Factor" is constructed over the course of years and can become an essential catalyst in propelling them to heights beyond the athletic arena into paths unimaginable!

The mental edge of competition, excellence, and accomplishment is ever-present, whether it be an entrepreneurial endeavor, a career with a great company, or even coaching.

Finding the Balance

Many athletes who transitioned from sports to another career (or any non-athletic endeavor) attest that it was difficult to shift scales from the physical to the mental.

They find that what used to come so easy for them in their athletic giftedness takes a shift in the world of career success or business competition. It's weighted by less physical attributes or bravado and more team strategy, mental prowess, and people skills.

Imagine what it would be like to be an athlete. Envision shooting a three-pointer with two seconds left in a basketball game and the crowd going wild. So now, imagine transitioning out of that excitement, out of sports.

When The CHEERING Stops...

When I finally hung up my cleats and came into corporate America, the most significant transition was going from the physical game, which was more predominant, to the mental game.

You may ask, "Doesn't it take a strong mental game to be successful in sports?" Yes, but it takes a back seat to your physical body. So now you have to work on improving your mental game and communications. Generally, those who have mastered the game in their head and their bodies rise to the superstar level.

I often view our lives like a rocket ship on the launching pad. It expends almost three-quarters of its fuel when it's leaving the launch pad. As it soars higher into the atmosphere, it starts to drop off pieces along the way. This means, like the rocket, there are stages in life like your teachers, coaches, parents, or even your haters. They can help move you to get lift-off. And eventually, those pieces have to break off, and you have to do it on your own.

Along the way, you have to draw back on those things that these stages or people taught you. I realize the importance of having people that encourage, influence inspire and instruct you.

So let the media and the fans build the pedestals, but let us, as the athletes or former athletes, build the foundations and bridges to stand on and walk across. As we construct these thoroughfares and decide to walk across them, it is incumbent upon us to be open to new experiences, opportunities, and directions in our lives. When we are, we can deal with "When the CHEERING Stops" and we are ready to enter the next phase of our life.

Knowing how to Release

Far too often, athletes do not recognize the untapped reservoir of potential and latent ability built up within them through the years of wins and failures, not necessarily in that order.

Are you an active athlete? Whether you're in high school, college, or a pro, always think three to four moves ahead of where you are right now. Then, at some point, you must entertain and plan towards the next challenge for yourself beyond the goal post, past the court and the baseball diamond.

There are many transferrable skills from athletics to the business world. Companies love former athletes, particularly those who can exude confidence and competitiveness in the business world.

It's of vital importance to *strike while the iron is hot*. The shelf life of your skills, talents, and abilities has a timeline or a stopwatch attached.

Always keep in mind that it may be your name, honors, and lauded sports resume that gets you a job interview, but it may also depend on who you know. As Roger Staubach, the Dallas

When The CHEERING Stops...

Cowboy/Pro-Football Hall of Fame great once told me, "It's my football name that may have gotten me in the door to businesses , but it was the results that proved I could deliver time and time again that caused me to win!"

The 1951 fairytale film *Alice in Wonderland* has a very applicable and iconic scene in children's books. Alice encounters the Cheshire Cat along the road and asks, ***"Would you tell me which way I ought to go from here?"***

The Cheshire Cat says, ***"That depends a good deal on where you want to get to."***

That statement is as applicable for the transitioning athlete as Alice in the story. If you don't know where you're going or how to get there, any route will do. It reminds me of an old strategy I've adopted for my own life in terms of moving forward.

Lastly, I would be remiss if I didn't include this little *five-letter word* that held so many athletes in their pursuit of life or destiny back: PRIDE. Pride solidifies the glue of inertia, so people live stuck lives. It's both a strength and a weakness. The same pride that allowed you to execute, perform your best, and succeed can also bring you to a standstill if you don't ask for help. In asking, you get the benefit of Education, Exposure, and Leverage

When The CHEERING Stops...

Transitioning from Field to Life

Transitions are an inevitable part of life. Once we are in position we have to then decide on how we are going to respond to a transition (movement of position).

Transitions occur in every living human being's life, but the transition of an athlete has fascinating parallels. Athletes become so married to their sport that having to leave it tears against their fabric. They have devoted their life to their sport, yet are required to move forward!

Transitioning is never easy for someone who always looks forward and betterment of their life, but can be if we are comfortable, being, doing, and having something you would prefer holding on to.

To transition doesn't mean you are at a standstill waiting for something to happen. You are taking action, but it's all designed to get you from one place to another. It doesn't take feelings into account because some or most transitions are not painless, they require something of us. As I mentioned earlier, to successfully transition out of sports, no matter the sport, you must first and foremost *DEVELOP A PLAN*.

When The CHEERING Stops...

No one wants to fail, but no planning places your odds of failure at a very high percentage.

Now I know a lot of athletes who don't like to plan but love and thrive on their spontaneity, but even they practice in their head the moves, the defenses, and the audible they would call if confronted with change, or transition.

Great athletes must constantly evolve and adjust their game! The truth is having an option or two never hurt anybody, but too many options can create distractions, and they will always diminish your results. I speak all over the country, and constantly tell my audiences to get a jump start on life.

Every athlete needs a "going forward "plan (not a backup plan). When you're going forward, you are transitioning, it indicates movement, and movement is a good work ethic. People constantly say "man, it's always good to have a backup plan," and I would agree, but take caution in not allowing your backup plan to become a "just in case plan."

Try to make sure it doesn't become a premature safety net that could generate a mental block preventing you from giving yourself totally to the If you are an athlete reading this book and you have a dream, you owe it to yourself to give it all you got!

When The CHEERING Stops...

I recall my rookie year after being drafted by the Cleveland Browns and attending spring NFL camps (there were no combines). The coaching staff designed these camps to see what type of athletes they really drafted, and get a glimpse of you close up to see your skillset and determine if you had a shot at making the team in training camp.

I'll never forget right before leaving Los Angeles going to Cleveland, I met Butch Johnson, a receiver for the Dallas Cowboys at a field he trained at in is Los Angeles. He told me, "When you go to training camp, take over and let them know from day one, that you came not to leave."

So I stopped in my hometown of Kansas City, Missouri, to shop for a large steamer trunk (not used much today). I loaded everything pretty much that I owned and packed it in that trunk, and when arriving at rookie training camp, all the rookies asked me while checking into the dorms, "Man, why did you bring that big trunk? You act like you moving in." I told them because I don't plan on leaving, so I packed everything I had."

You see, I didn't have a backup plan, because I was so focused on my goal, I didn't want the distractions of "what if" to enter my mind. My backup plan was birthed in the classroom, developing a name for myself in sports at USC, and meeting alumni that one day might hire me or help me move to the next level.

"Isaac, I don't know if I'll get a scholarship or not. I mean I love this game of football, have been playing it all my life, in the streets, pop warner, middle school, the whole nine, sent film, everything, but nobody is offering me a scholarship." Mike said, "Isaac, you are a real good athlete, but you also have some other great qualities, you're a leader, people like you, a great student, you have what it takes, it will work out somehow."

You might be Mike in the story and were a decent high school athlete, and you find yourself in a place, whether it's when high school sports are over, and no one is waiving a four-year scholarship your way, or maybe college is nearing its end, and you're wondering what the next steps are?

First, we need to examine the statistics. Only 2.3% of all high school players in this country become college players! And out of the 9000 players that make it to the college level, only 215 will ever make an NFL roster.

Don't get me wrong, I always wanted to be one of the ones in that 2.3 % and part of the 215 players, and because you probably love a challenge, you owe it to yourself to give it all you got! So plan in advance to go beyond your sports life when the odds sometimes say "no, "That's a lesson on faith and belief for another time."

Unless you were a starter on a professional football team, your job was up for grabs every year. If you were a person who didn't have an NFL resume, the opportunities were fewer. So that's when I finally realized that the "cheering had stopped" for me in football, and trying out another year would be futile.

For example, a few years ago I had a conversation with a young athlete who was trying to break into the NFL. He was an undrafted player but good enough to get invited to an NFL combine to be evaluated by various NFL teams. Just to be invited said something about his overall ability, but as luck had it, he was not called to training camp and had spent the last three years campaigning to get another tryout. He wrote letters, sent resumes and video clips to draw the attention of NFL coaches and teams.

So I mentioned him to my wife and I told her ""Sonia if this kid would put this kind of effort in finding a job in a company or start his own business, he would be wildly successful!"

Many athletes suffer from one problem: we believe that we have "all the time in the world" to prepare, get ready, or adjust to changing conditions. As athletes, we should be like our coaches, always planning for contingencies, new defenses, or offenses that come up against our game plans.

Once you have developed a plan, now it's time to take the step that most tend to leave out, and that's "take inventory!" Take inventory just as you would if you owned a company that had various goods and products in your warehouse. Only these are not as much physical as they are products made up of your past experiences, knowledge, skills, education, contacts, and financial resources, maybe even the dreams you have been carrying around inside of you for years, but never had the opportunity to release.

We all tend to focus on the now, until one day through loss, failure, or even devastation, we are forced to look at ourselves in the future of what could be and determine what we really bring to the table. So why is it we only make these life assessments when we have had to deal with loss? That answer is easy, we refuse to quit. Great athletes that have been tested and tempered through the fire of competition refuse to quit and throw in the towel, even when it's obvious to others. We refuse to accept it All of us believe that we have one more hooray, one more down, and one more play left in us.

When The CHEERING Stops...

Take personal inventory before circumstances force you to do so, and keep it in your playbook for future use!

I speak with a lot of athletes today who are no longer playing sports, and many don't recognize the absolute "goldmine "that is resident within them!

It's like a mine full of treasure inside of them that consists of untapped potential, untapped skills, and resources that can reach beyond the athletic field, pushing past the physical or keen athletic prowess they have always relied upon.

It is found in the rich deposits forged and pressed over time. Deposits of teamwork, consistent work ethic, victory, defeat, sacrifice, and continual discomfort on and off the field of play that creates a "diamond cutting tool" allowing that player to extract the treasure, process it, and present it to a world that's waiting!

Steven Covey, one of America's most renowned experts in human achievement and productivity, wrote a blockbuster book many years ago called *"The 7 Habits of Highly Effective People."* In that book he refers to a term called "sharpening the saw" because you can't carve out a magnificent future using a dull blade.

When The CHEERING Stops...

Any highly skilled athlete worth their salt knows that he must always sharpen his skills and knowledge of his sport to have a shot at success and longevity. You have to approach your transition similarly. As you begin addressing these questions, take the following actions:

1) List Your Past Experiences & Successes that may have prepared you for where you want to go next!

2) Access your suitability from past experiences so you can quickly extract the good and learn from the bad. Because whether in sports or after sports, bad experiences, coupled with life lessons, always serves to make you stronger.

As an athlete it's important that you tune in to what your experiences and successes say about you, because sometimes they will lie on you. They will tell you something about yourself that has long since passed. So to prevent this from overtaking you, I suggest immediately taking the next step.

You see inside this young man's mountain are treasures, traits, and characteristics that the world needs, but right now, he's attempting to eat at the wrong table. You see, his cheering stopped for him at the collegiate level, yet he hasn't been mining the resources inside.

When The CHEERING Stops...

Thoughts for Your Next Quarter

I shared before how important discipline is in the life of an athlete. All athletes incorporate levels of discipline in their lives. The great athletes who have separated themselves from the rest have successfully mastered discipline. However, I have seen athletes I grew up with have tremendous athletic ability but absolutely no discipline.

As I stated earlier, I bet if you could sit down and ask the greats in any sport, "What's the most important element in your game?" They would have to say DISCIPLINE. We can take someone like the legendary Tiger Woods. His father wrote a book called *Raising the Tiger*. He shared that the discipline he instilled in Tiger Woods didn't happen overnight. It was contoured, shaped, and developed over time until it became an instinct. Any person that achieves greatness has this type of discipline.

So whether you're entirely leaving the sports career or moving to a different area of sports, the same applies with one difference. It would help if you shifted from just disciplining your body to disciplining and educating your mind.

There has to be a discipline of your emotions and mind regarding your passions, ego, and integrity. More importantly, those with great passion often do things beyond their ability, but they still discipline themselves to guard what catches their eye and their heart. This discipline keeps them from going and doing things that will take them off course and aren't right for them.

Another area that I mentioned is disciplining your ego. All of us have egos. But we must discipline our egos in regards to ethics. Many athletes are considered role models, so it's vitally important to discipline ourselves ethically. Unfortunately, today we find a lack of ethics in sports. Egos have destroyed more families, companies, and relationships than you can imagine. If we're not ready to discipline our egos for something greater than ourselves, then we're headed for a fall.

It moves even to the level of sportsmanship. As you break the word down, *"it's sports manning the ship."* I've seen so many athletes walk right off the court or field without shaking their competitor's hand or even speaking when they have lost the game or contest. Sportsmanship is doing it even if you don't feel like it. There are many times that I've lost a game, meet, or race, and because I had disciplined my ego, I stopped to shake the hands of my opponents. As you move to other areas of your life, you will have to do things you don't want to.

When The CHEERING Stops...

Discipline will build you a bridge to cross instead of a wall to climb over. Discipline will prepare you for your purpose so that if you get off track, you're able to get right back on. Oftentimes, there's that voice in your head telling you it's all over, you can't go on, or that you can't be successful. Well, that voice is lying to you. Instead, tell yourself, "I remember what it's like to be disciplined." And that's when you have to engage and reach out to your coach, mentor, or spiritual leader.

They'll help you strengthen your discipline so you don't give up, back down, or walk away. My coaches helped shape my character and my work ethic. I had a strong foundation from working with my Uncle on the farm. It evolved from there to a whole new level for the field. I read in the scripture to train up a child in the way they should go, and when they're old, they won't depart. So parents have a responsibility to train, and coaches have a responsibility to develop. But the key element is walking and living it out. We have to learn how to reach out beyond our comfort zones to those who can help us get to the next level.

Along the way, every athlete reaches a time in their career when they struggle to reach their peak performance. For example, a receiver that has gotten rusty in running their routes against their opponent. When the wide receiver cuts the route, it means the quarterback is not ready to throw the ball, and it will mess up

131

the timing up of the route. So, they have to discipline themselves to get back to that place of precision.

My Next Quarter - Corporate Job

I was the first offensive player drafted by the Cleveland Browns, in the 7th round of a 12th round draft, excited and confident to be competing for a spot on an NFL roster.

Unfortunately, I was cut with one game left in the preseason. It was a crushing blow to my ego because I had a real solid preseason, basically catching everything thrown to me and alternating time playing behind the Browns' All-Pro starting wide-receiver Paul Warfield.

Even though I was disappointed in not making the final Browns roster, I knew inside that I was still good enough to play in the NFL, if ever given a real opportunity again.

I sat that time staying in shape, re-running the tape in my head, reliving, rethinking, and retooling my game to be ready for another shot.

During that time something stuck with me. I remembered from my first cousin, who was never one to be shy about expressing her mind, saying:

When The CHEERING Stops...

"You know cousin, up to this point, being a Pro hasn't totally worked out your way, so in case you don't make it in the pros, have something else to fall back on."

That was the last thing I wanted to hear, yet the very thing that I needed to hear, and I never forgot.

Not long after that, I landed an interview with IBM. Not too far into the meeting, the sales manager or recruiter said, "Kenny, I like you and believe you could be a fit here, but I can tell you still have football in your blood. So here's my advice, go back and give it another shot, and when the day comes that you have gotten football out of your system, come back and see us. We'll have a job for you."

Well, that day came sooner than expected. Three and a half years later, I said goodbye to competitive sports, the unique camaraderie, and the addictive passion that had engulfed my life for the past 12 years.

My second encounter with IBM came when some former Dallas Cowboy teammates suggested we apply for positions with IBM in the offseason. Unfortunately, the company didn't have part-time jobs, not even for Pro Football players. Even though we had heard that they liked quality candidates with athletic backgrounds.

So, I filled out an application, waited to be contacted, and nothing happened. One weekend I went to Houston to visit my girlfriend and attended a party at a-n UT Alum's home that a Marketing Manager for IBM attended. Once we spoke about my interest and the application submitted, he made a few calls and my application was sped up for an interview. Within one week, I was in Houston for an interview. Low and behold, I was offered a sales position in IBM's Large Systems Division.

Many might say you must have had some smarts to work for that prestigious company. I say no, I was willing to engage people from all points of the spectrum and leverage relationships. That's why I was offered the opportunity to be heard. The rest was up to me.

Leveraged Relationships

I got my first job because I accepted a position with another company that was expecting me to work for them in Houston. My high school football coach was coaching the running backs at the University of Texas, and he knew a prominent alumni at UT, who was best friends with a marketing manager at IBM.

Fortunately, the manager was impressed enough that he called the company and got me an interview, and within two weeks I was hired and accepted the position.

Always remember that relationships are a gift, and the old adage is true *"it's not always what you know that gets you in the door. It's who you know that can open that door that counts most."*

Finding My Place

It's not always easy finding your place when you've had your heart set on continuing the thing you've done so well for so long. You may find yourself learning a whole new profession, a whole new way of thinking, or a whole new way of competing. That's not intimidating. You're just learning to play a "new sport" called business.

Yes, you will have to work to find your place and your rhythm. I now know that I wasn't in my final place of success, but it was undoubtedly a great start. Once you get a great start towards something that provides opportunity then that opportunity will offer momentum. Once momentum is in effect, you will see a faster track to the success you seek.

Once that has been obtained, it may lead you to a springboard for more oopportunities. Leading you to find that rhythm I keep speaking about and pave the way for success at a much greater level.

135

Internationally famous singer/songwriter Stevie Wonder wrote a song many years ago called "Place in the Sun."

> *"There's a place in the sun where's there's hope for everyone , where my poor restless heart got to run, there a place in the sun and before my life is done got to find me a place in the sun..."*

When you finally find your place in the sun, then maybe you can start to repeat the patterns of success experienced in sports, only now transferring it to a new arena.

When it came to finding my place, I know from experience that it took a series of different jobs in a single industry that probably was not best suited for my skills and gifting.

Yet because I was so competitive, I was determined to stick it out and make it work no matter the obstacles. That was the mindset I needed to overcome and finally come into my new season in the sun.

Earning My Place

When I was a freshman in college, the school newspaper wrote an article on me. Because I had come into the university as both a high school football and track star, the hopes were that I would continue in that vein and become a two-sport success in college as well.

The article was entitled, **"Kenny Randle: A Study in Determination"**

I never forgot that article because it exemplified how I lived my life. I lived life determined to succeed, determined to win, determined to survive and overcome whatever came my way. Which probably came from my neighborhood training in that lot.

I'm reminded of a saying my pastor, Bishop TD Jakes, quotes and still shares in his messages that states: *"It doesn't matter how you start, it only matters how you finish."* All too often people are stopped by their start. If it wasn't glamorous or stellar, they tend to denigrate and demean it. They convince themselves that since they didn't start well, they won't end well. The important thing to know is you can start slow or poorly yet still win big because you finish well. It's the finish that makes the difference.

Therefore earning my place was just a matter of never giving up and continuing to believe in myself. It took praying, trusting, and searching for those willing to assist me in my quest for success. I am still amazed at the number of people that came in the circle to assist me to find my victory at this next level!

What is the mindset you have right now reading this book? Are you determined to win at all costs? Of course, it must be done honestly and legally. Maybe you've been disillusioned, feel stuck, or feel like you never truly have made that transition? You must have BELIEF and DETERMINATION! So don't ever give up, help is on the way. The resources are not hidden from you, but hidden for you to discover.

Marriage and Family

Before getting married, I recall telling my closest circle of football buddies that I would be married within two years from when we spoke. They laughed "how in the world can you say that's going to happen in two years? " Why two years? I shared with them, "because I'm going to settle down and begin squeezing people out of my black book that don't need to be there causing problems, bringing situations, interference, or misunderstanding. I had been running with a bunch of pro-athletes who constantly were in the fast lane. I knew that lane and pace would fade out soon, so I began to prepare for it.

Well, two years went by, I had transitioned out of football, and moved from Dallas to Houston. I got married, and a new phase of my life as a newlywed began to take shape. Of course, I would be exaggerating to say that everything found its perfect place and rhythm now that we were married.

We had known one another since high school. Her father was my gym teacher in 7th and 8th grade. He was tough as nails and shot fear in the hearts of most boys in the city who would dare think about dating or stepping up to his daughter. But, I liked her enough to confront that reality and didn't let that fear or intimidation deter me.

We were married ten years before we had our first child. No doubt to those around us, she was our miracle baby. We had been trying for so long to have children and found ourselves constantly trying everything to no avail until one weekend at a marriage retreat. It totally shifted the course of our lives.

We received a prophetic word from a pastor about our personal lives that only God, my wife, and I could have possibly known. Within 60 days after that meeting, my wife became pregnant with our first daughter. Our second daughter came when we moved back to Dallas.

Going into marriage was a major life shift and commitment. That is probably why it took me so long to get there, not because I didn't desire marriage, but because I wanted it to

139

work. Divorce was not an option for me as it was not experienced in my family tree.

We had a limited knowledge of how to raise kids. We decided to raise them with a combination of how both of our families raised us. What we didn't know we gleaned from others, we sought the Lord's advice and followed His word. *"To train up children in the way that they should go, so that they do not depart"* I know that sounds too simple, but over the years we have trusted it to be effective.

"OMG, what faith, discipline, and growth that required to do it right! Neither my wife nor I came from families with a lot of financial success, certainly not mine. I came from a single-parent home where my Mom struggled much of the time. My mother was young and wanted nice things, but she was too much of a spender.

On the other hand my wife's Mom was a teacher, and although she planned, saved and paid bills on time, there were other struggles in the house. So you can imagine when we came into our marriage, we had different experiences and thoughts we had to merge and reconcile.

When my wife and I got married, we set a course to succeed financially. We availed ourselves to every workshop or seminar about making money but not managing it.

When The CHEERING Stops...

We had the best intentions but made wrong career moves, and entrepreneurial ventures left us in a position of frequent need. In the background, I availed myself of every self-help and money management book I could get my hands on to gain some direction. We believed by faith that God would bless us financially as a family if we availed ourselves to solid financial principles and remained good stewards over what he had placed in our hands.

Although we followed and believed biblical principles regarding finances, I had to grow and learn through my failures, inadequacies, and shortcomings to be prepared for a much bigger purpose related to our faith and finances.

The things that I've written up to this point, educated and developed my faith in God.

I remember a quote from Robert F. Kennedy that said, *"Some men see things as they are and ask why? I dream things that never were and ask why not?"*

I believe that faith allows you to see the unseen, until it becomes the seen. The scriptures say ***faith is the substance of things hoped for and the evidence of things not Seen.***

Believe it or not, I still have faith in the common good of mankind, not to go down but become better. Although today we see that many of our treasured foundations seem to be crumbling all around us. I believe that faith and possibly blind faith strengthens us not to lose heart. We must tell ourselves that we can do more to make a difference on this earth.

Me and the Marketplace

My Marketplace Journey has been interesting and different from most. From the time I entered the business world, I knew nothing except wanting to succeed. There was an ache inside of me that wanted to win no matter what. I have always had a competitive spirit, and winning was in my DNA.

I guess it has always been my nature to absorb different realms of experiences, exposure, ecstasy or endorphins of successes along the way, and learn from my failures.

Oh, no doubt if I could, I would change some bad decisions I made along the way. Yet I count it all joy because it allowed me to gain the life lessons that came from the paths taken. That has allowed me to commit and develop myself in such a way to leave a legacy for my children and others to follow. I have learned invaluable lessons along the way.

To transition to the next level takes a great deal of focus and discipline. Many people look for the secret weapon, silver bullet or the secret sauce of success and life. They attribute it to how smart, talented, or connected the person succeeding is compared to themselves.

It has been my experience after seeing, experiencing, and connecting with very successful people throughout my life that those traits and attributes are valuable. But I have discovered that it boils down to their focus and discipline.

Mr. or Ms. Athlete, trace it back to your Sports lineage, and you will realize that the one thing that separated you from the rest, outside of skill and ability, was your focus and your discipline to be successful

I was never much for climbing the corporate ladder, even when I went to work at the IBM Corporation, one of the largest companies in the world at the time. I wasn't willing to pay the cost to climb the corporate ladder or play the necessary games to move up. Yet some people were very comfortable with that process. I take my hat off to them as they were very successful in that role.

I will be the first to tell you, climbing the corporate ladder of success is not a game for the weak at heart. Especially in large corporations where politics, positioning, one-upmanship, and cutthroat competition exist inside its inner sanctum. Even smaller companies have some of these dynamics. It's just human nature to compete and want to get ahead. But, after doing it for so long, you tend to look for something more meaningful or more impactful.

Run your own Race

What I'm really saying is be true to yourself. What is your race, your focus? I'm not asking about your ethnicity. It's about your focus.

Your race has to be one that you have a rhythm to run in an outstanding manner. Just like athletics, you must train to build your knowledge or stamina. You must be willing to line up to the starting line and give it your best race each and every day.

Lastly, I would be disingenuous if I didn't express or share with you the role God has played in my journey. I grew up in a God-fearing home. In my house, if you weren't God-fearing, my mother had a way of striking the fear of God in you. That's a fact!

I have always been a believer in the gospel message. It was taught to me over and over as a kid. Yet as I grew older, the application of living it out became fuzzy. It had little impact on me while in college or professional sports.

One day, some of my Dallas Cowboy teammates invited me to a Bible study. A linebacker by the name of Guy Brown invited me. After it was over, I walked out of the meeting saying, "That was nice, but these guys are a little fanatical." I only attended one time, but the atmosphere stayed with me.

Three years later, when I lived in Houston I joined a local church. But, if I recall my own story correctly, one evening, I had left the church, got to my home, and found myself praying, repenting, and calling unto God for Him to come into my life in a stronger way.

Can I tell you "that God never forgets?" As I found myself on my knees reaching out to Him, the Spirit of God spoke to my heart. It was not an audible voice, yet I heard it in my heart "do you remember when you walked out of that Bible study in Dallas and said it was good, but they were fanatical?" I answered in my heart, "yes."

You see, God will speak to something you can understand. He went on to say, "you didn't think it was fanatical when 85,000 people were in the stands, yelling, screaming, cheering, drinking, and painting themselves in their team colors. You didn't call that fanatical, did you?"

God forgets nothing. The next thing He spoke to my heart as a reminder was, "the reason you thought that they were fanatical was that you didn't have a personal relationship with me, and they had one." That night I drew my heart closer to God, and it changed me forever. To this day, every time I see my former teammate in Dallas, I thank him.

Now, you're entitled to your opinion for those who debate or doubt whether I heard from God. As I said, there was no audible voice, no skies parting, no handwriting in the sky, but He spoke to my heart. It all came in a flash, not a long drawn-out conversation. Just so you know, I have been a licensed minister for over 22 years and would not hesitate to tell you in no uncertain terms that I would rather defend an experience from God than debate an opinion any day!

As I grew in my relationship and understanding, I made God my senior partner in every business deal and every opportunity. That said, I 'm not trying to convert you, but I want to open up your heart to God's desire to orchestrate and help you in your business affairs.

In essence, I'm a Christian businessman. I have had countless instances in my business where I was truly at the right place and right time because of God. I know it had nothing to do with me but everything to do with Him.

When The CHEERING Stops...

New Found Field of Play

There is a newfound feeling to play today in the world of business. In this ever-complex technological marketplace we live in that can change every moment, where real relationships in business are becoming somewhat robotic and distant.

We have to be careful not to take the "human" out of human resources. As technology and social media has advanced, we must also learn to advance our ways of connecting and creating solid business relationships that are enduring, endearing, and valuable to the business world of the future.

I'm sure you've heard this a thousand times, but it is worth repeating. When I left sports I really didn't have a long-term vision, but I had a long-term goal. I knew that whatever I put my mind to do it with all my heart and all my might, and if it was the right endeavor I would succeed.

In closing, I need to mention something I stated earlier. To make that transition "when the cheering stops" focus on the following steps:

#1: Decide what you want

#2 Decide what you're willing to give up to get what

#3 Associate with those who can help you get what you want

#4 Plan your work and work your plan

It's so important to decide exactly what you want. Even if it's temporary. Because doing so allows you to make a decision, and move forward. You can always adjust or reset later.

If you choose not to develop a plan for your life, there will always be someone who will have a plan for you. Treat your business, career, or life goals the same way you did your athletic career. Make sure your plans are always bold, stretching and challenging you to be your optimum self!

I believe I set my sights too low when I started in corporate America because I really didn't know what I wanted. It was all foreign soil to me. Now you see why having a mentor can be so valuable. All I had been taught was to go to school, get a good education, get a good job, and you could expect to have success.

That was only part of the equation because the question that needed to be answered was, "what was a good job?" When I searched for what I thought was a good job, it actually helped me acquire skills to become better and propel myself to the next opportunity.

148

When The CHEERING Stops...

I realize that the jobs I had previous to what I do now prepared me for a walk, calling, and career like none I could have envisioned. We have to remember that the business career path like life is not a sprint but a marathon with many stations along the way to refresh, renovate or redefine.

I ended up with a lot of mid-term goals in areas I thought would give me financial success or financial freedom. I thought being in my own business could produce its own success. Being able to chart my own course was important to me. I wanted something to get me through everything, just like I did on the field.

Many of the exploits I pursued were temporary or small successes. Yet, when I look back, I realize that the desire was there, but the vehicle I was looking for had not been discovered yet.

I never had a problem deciding what I was willing to give up. I was always loyal and dedicated to that which I believed. That's why I use my business platform for ministry. I'm not only dedicated to helping businesses and business people, I'm dedicated to enhancing others' lives. It gives me great joy and great privilege to see how the power of God changes people's lives and businesses for the better.

When The CHEERING Stops...

"We're now crossing the Grand Canyon," the pilot announced over the PA system as we cruised across a cloudless sky at 33,000 ft. The concert of "oooohs" and "aaahhs" made by the passengers sounded like a group of eight-year-old kids in front of a glass window at a candy store.

I was flying to Los Angeles to reunite with a group of men whose combined talents and God-given athletic abilities won the NCAA Track & Field Championship at the famous Penn Track Stadium in Philadelphia (home of the Penn Relays). To my knowledge, it had been well over 25 years since the school had won that honor in the men's division.

When I first received the invitation to attend, I wasn't sure I had the time, considering my business schedule and prevailing ministry commitments. Then a call came from one of my best friends, Guy Abraham, and nailed it for me.

"You are going to attend the reunion, right?" He said in his patented high-pitched Panamanian voice that always raced 90 miles an hour. You know you were the captain, right?" My lack of a quick response was a dead giveaway that I really had not made plans or a concerted effort to be there.

Guy shared the importance of my being there as only he could describe. The memories of that time in history and our relationship as friends began to unfold in my mind again. I guess my sense of obligation rose in me. Probably more heavily in the desire department, because I suppose, deep down inside, it was one more opportunity to bask in the glory of the crowd, be it small or large. I told him that I had thought about it but had made no plans to be at the reunion.

And here I was, heading to the University of Southern California. In my heart and probably thoughts, it seemed to be just "One More Reach for Glory." Ultimately, after that reunion, I was inducted into the USC hall of fame for track and field, which was a great honor in my athletic career.

As I stood at that event with my family in attendance, I was surprised to see four of my business associates there. They had decided to surprise me by flying from Dallas, Houston, San Antonio, and California. They used their own resources to get there and honor me. It goes to show that authentic relationships are often forged beyond the field.

That was a special day that still resonates in my spirit far more than much of the cheering I left behind. They were there because of our friendship in business, which became my new team and competitive field of play.

When The CHEERING Stops...

So there is hope *"When the Cheering Stops."* There is a whole new world to be discovered and a whole new you that the world needs to discover.

Life begins ***WHEN THE CHEERING STOPS!***

About the Author

Kenny Randle is an entrepreneur, writer, public speaker, business consultant, and CEO of Global Community Outreach, a Dallas-based entity. He has over 25 years as a successful executive in human resource outsourcing strategies and solutions across multiple industries for small to medium-sized businesses.

Kenny began his business career after performing as a World-class track and field athlete and a short stint in the NFL, with the Dallas Cowboys and the Cleveland Browns.

When The CHEERING Stops...

He attended the University of Southern California (USC), on a football and track scholarship, playing on two National Championship Football and Track & Field Teams. He graduated with a BS in Marketing from the Marshall School of Business.

A high achiever and dedicated community servant, Kenny has served on various boards in the Dallas Metroplex, including the Make-A-Wish Foundation, The Entrepreneur Institute (TEI), The Metroplex Economic Development Corporation, and mentored for several years in DISD Middle School. He currently serves on the board for The Positive Coaching Alliance (PCA), an organization providing character education and mentorship for youth sports.

Kenny is a licensed minister and Elder at The Potter's House Church in Dallas, Texas, a 30,000 member congregation under the leadership of Bishop T.D. Jakes. He serves as a member of the teaching faculty of The Potter's House School of Ministry, and Director of the Men's Ministry, whose mission focuses on empowering, equipping, and discipling men for 21st Century Impact.

Made in the USA
Monee, IL
18 April 2023

32057578R00085